PEEPSHOW
Praise for the series:

It was only a matter of time before
is an audience for whom *Exile ∙*
are as significant and worthy of
Middlemarch . . . The series . . . is fr∙
minute rock-geek analysis to i∙
— *The New York*

Ideal for the rock geek who thi∙
— *Roll∙*

One of the coolest publishing imprints on the planet — *Bookslut*

These are for the insane collectors out there who appreciate fantastic
design, well-executed thinking, and things that make your house look cool.
Each volume in this series takes a seminal album and breaks it down in
startling minutiae. We love these. We are huge nerds — *Vice*

A brilliant series . . . each one a work of real love — *NME* (UK)

Passionate, obsessive, and smart — *Nylon*

Religious tracts for the rock 'n' roll faithful — *Boldtype*

[A] consistently excellent series — *Uncut* (UK)

We . . . aren't naive enough to think that we're your only source for reading
about music (but if we had our way . . . watch out). For those of you who
really like to know everything there is to know about an album, you'd do
well to check out Bloomsbury's "33⅓" series of books — *Pitchfork*

**For reviews of individual titles in the series, please visit our blog
at 333sound.com and our website at http://www.bloomsbury.com/
musicandsoundstudies**

Follow us on Twitter: @333books

Like us on Facebook: https://www.facebook.com/33.3books

For a complete list of books in this series, see the back of this book.

Forthcoming in the series:

and many more …

Peepshow

Peepshow

Samantha Bennett

BLOOMSBURY ACADEMIC
NEW YORK · LONDON · OXFORD · NEW DELHI · SYDNEY

BLOOMSBURY ACADEMIC
Bloomsbury Publishing Inc
1385 Broadway, New York, NY 10018, USA
50 Bedford Square, London, WC1B 3DP, UK

BLOOMSBURY, BLOOMSBURY ACADEMIC and the Diana logo are
trademarks of Bloomsbury Publishing Plc

First published in the United States of America 2019

Cover design: 333sound.com

Bloomsbury Publishing Inc does not have any control over, or
responsibility for, any third-party websites referred to or in this book.
All internet addresses given in this book were correct at the time of going
to press. The author and publisher regret any inconvenience caused if
addresses have changed or sites have ceased to exist, but can accept no
responsibility for any such changes.

A catalog record for this book is available from the Library of Congress.

ISBN: PB: 978-1-5013-2186-3
ePDF: 978-1-5013-2185-6
eBook: 978-1-5013-2187-0

Series: 33$\frac{1}{3}$

Typeset by Deanta Global Publishing Services, Chennai, India
Printed and bound in the United States of America

To find out more about our authors and books visit www.bloomsbury.com
and sign up for our newsletters.

Contents

Track Listing

1. Peek-A-Boo [3.10]
2. The Killing Jar [4.04]
3. Scarecrow [5.06]
4. Carousel [4.25]
5. Burn-Up [4.32]
6. Ornaments of Gold [3.49]
7. Turn to Stone [4.05]
8. Rawhead and Bloodybones [2.29]
9. The Last Beat of My Heart [4.29]
10. Rhapsody [6.24]

mise en scène

[MRS. STEPHENS] Take me to your cinema.
— *Peeping Tom*

[JEFF]: You mean that you can explain everything strange
that has been going on over there, and is still going on?
[Lt. DOYLE]: No, and neither can you. That's a secret
private world you're looking into out there.
— *Rear Window*

[STEVE] What does it all look like to you?
[MOTORCYCLE BOY] Black and white TV with the
sound turned low.
— *Rumble Fish*

[WILL HALLOWAY] Somewhere, not far back, was a
terrible storm.
— *Something Wicked This Way Comes*

Originating in theater, the French term *mise en scène* directly translates as "setting the stage" and is used to describe the organization of visual elements and the "contents of the frame"[1] in film: the position of the actors; props and scenery; costumes; lighting; and, critically, the interactions between actors, both as acted and interpreted by an audience.[2] In the immediate aftermath of the 1987 Great Storm, Siouxsie and the Banshees left cosmopolitan London for their pre-production *scéne*: Berry House, situated in the fourteenth-century parish of Ardingly and nestled in the heart of Sussex High Weald woodland.

It is not surprising that the band would consistently reference this striking rural location as having a significant impact on *Peepshow*'s aesthetic direction. The deracinated landscape of torn up woodland,[3] coupled with evening and nighttime recording in this seventeenth-century farmhouse, evoked the *mise en scène* of the very film that inspired the band's name in the first place: that of Gordon Hessler's British occult horror, *Cry of the Banshee* (1970). Film studies scholar Marcus Harmes suggested that *Cry of the Banshee* "inhabit[s] a world defined by rural horror. The photography lingers over shots of fields, woods, and villages"[4] and "despite its seventeenth-century setting, *[Cry of the] Banshee* was filmed around Grim's Dyke, a Victorian manor house."[5] Grim's Dyke is one of many examples of the haunted house as cinematic anchor; a building synonymous with trepidation, darkness, hidden secrets, and the aura of the past. As Barbara Creed suggested, "The house is horrifying not simply because of its appearance (dark, dank, empty, slimy, mysterious, foreboding) but also because of the crimes committed within a familial context."[6]

The haunted house is a common cinematic motif, usually situated in woodland surrounds, often depicted at night, most of the time in conjunction with bad weather: thick fog, storms, and/or driving rain. This clichéd *mise en scène* plays out in the films of American International Pictures (AIP), particularly Roger Corman's *House of Usher* (1960) and another example is found in one of lead singer Siouxsie Sioux's favorite films,[7] James Whale's *The Old Dark House* (1932). A classic pastiche on this mainstay horror trope is found in Sharman's *The Rocky Horror Picture Show* (1975) in the scene where a naïve Janet sings "There's A Light (Over at the Frankenstein Place)" as she attempts to cover her hair from the pouring rain with newspaper while approaching Dr. Frank N. Furter's castle. Yet perhaps the most disturbing example is the Men's Association mansion house, the site of Joanna's death and automaton reincarnation in Bryan Forbes's *The Stepford Wives* (1975)— another film that influenced Sioux in myriad ways.[8] That the band's pre-production setting of Berry House was such a similarly evocative cinematic locality would undoubtedly inspire *Peepshow*'s filmic direction.

The environmental and cultural contrasts between urban London and the surrounding rural home counties are difficult to overstate. Once beyond the capital's border, the tube stations, dense Victorian terraces, smoggy skies, and black cabs vanish in an instant. The boundless North Downs roll out across the horizon like a green carpet, patterned with pretty woodland and patchwork fields. But in October 1987, the Great Storm had violently eviscerated the chocolate-box charm from the North Downs; Siouxsie and the Banshees' trip to the countryside was an ominous journey back in time, as Sioux recalled:

> There was an underlying sense of foreboding. A couple of weeks before leaving for Ardingly, the country had been devastated by huge, unprecedented storms. As we drove down there, we passed through a landscape ripped apart by all these fallen trees with their roots showing.[9]

The name "Berry House" derives from the Anglo Saxon "bury" meaning "fortified." Partly restructured, the large, country residence is an "Arts-and-Crafts" style building, very similar in size and surrounds to Hessler's Grim's Dyke. The neatly pruned gardens had been left in tatters after the storm as giant cedars crashed into the house, knocking its chimney stack from the roof.[10] Thick fog carpeted the grounds all the way to the horizon. Winds reaching speeds of 120 miles per hour decimated the National Grid, and on October 16, 1987, plunged London into a twenty-four-hour blackout. Country power lines took far longer to restore and those residing in the rural surrounds lived in eerie darkness for weeks. Studio manager Curtis Schwartz organized a giant electrical generator, positioned in the grounds of Berry House by an industrial crane.[11] The generator kept studio sessions ticking over, in spite of twice daily farm drives for the agricultural diesel required to power it. Inside the studio, an industrious and inspired Siouxsie and the Banshees rehearsed daily, layering up instruments to an AKAI twelve-track recorder, piecing together *Peepshow*'s lyrical narrative.[12]

In contrast to Sioux's sense of foreboding, the Banshees were relaxed, and reveled in a newfound "frivolity and craziness."[13]   Drummer Budgie and bassist-songwriter Steven Severin delighted in their discovery of White Shield home brew at a peculiar beverage shop, later instigating a yard-of-ale drinking contest at Berry House.[14] "It became more dangerous when we ran out of beer and started using this hardcore, eight percent fizzy cider,"[15] recalled newly recruited guitarist Jon Klein, the proud winner. (Incidentally, this was such a defining memory of the pre-production sessions that "Yardov Ail" is thanked in *Peepshow's* liner notes.) Long, drunken nights swilling intoxicating concoctions morphed into days of songwriting and production, broken with occasional outings to local antiques markets and a gypsy caravan park, where fairground music emanating from one of the caravans was recorded.[16]

Every November fifth, towns and villages across England commemorate the 1605 Gunpowder Plot: a foiled assassination attempt on King James I by provincial English Catholics. With spectacular fireworks displays and monumental bonfire processions, Sussex village(r)s celebrate "Guy Fawkes night" with notorious enthusiasm. Townsfolk gather excitedly in the streets. Faces glow in the light of spinning sparklers. The ancient ode to the perils of treason, *Remember, remember the fifth of November,* is fondly, yet nervously recited. Nearby Ardingly, the village of Lindfield has marked bonfire night every November fifth since 1881. Visitors flock from the surrounding towns for the renowned fireworks display and in 1987, Siouxsie and the Banshees broke their pre-production sessions for bonfire night festivities. Drunk on local ale and embracing his inner Viking, producer Mike Hedges staggered around yelling "rubbish!"[17] as local children marveled in awe at Roman candles exploding like gunshots. To the banging of drums and riotous—*murderous*—chants, a flaring torch procession played out the traitor's final journey as they paraded a fifteen-foot Guy Fawkes effigy through the village streets and toward the colossal bonfire.

Later, Sioux recalled the archaic, cult-like atmosphere at Ardingly: "It was as if we were doing the whole thing on the set of *The Wicker Man*."[18]

*   *   *

In 1980, Sioux confided to journalist Lucy O'Brien, "I'd like to star in a film with Bette Davis. I see myself like a light with music shining through me."[19] O'Brien later reflected, "I thought that was so profound I underlined it in my notebook right there and then."[20] O'Brien's recognition of the importance of such a statement was rare. Despite the deep filmic influences imbued in the band's twenty-year discography, this dimension of Siouxsie and the Banshees had—and has—yet to be fully explored. Starting from references to Frank Perry's *The Swimmer* (1968) on the band's debut *The Scream* (1978) to the Hitchcockian track "Spellbound" (1981). From the cover of the Sherman Brothers' "Trust in Me" (1967), taken from Walt Disney's *The Jungle Book* (1967) on *Through the Looking Glass* (1987), to the Jane Mansfield-inspired "Kiss Them For Me" (1991), this is a band whose love of film has long been ingrained in their repertoire. On their 2002 "Seven Year Itch" reunion tour, Siouxsie and the Banshees performed less a retrospective or "greatest hits" set and more a collection of songs exemplifying the filmic dimension of their music. Tracks from later and more mainstream albums *Superstition* (1991) and *The Rapture* (1995) were notably absent and instead, the band finished their set each night with the genre defying "Peek-A-Boo," as if this lead single from their ninth studio album *Peepshow* signified the highlight, the *pinnacle* of their career.

It was.

Peepshow was Siouxsie and the Banshees at their most musically accomplished creative peak, having consolidated their lineup of original Banshees—singer-songwriter Siouxsie Sioux and bassist-songwriter Steven Severin—and long-term drummer Budgie with ex-Specimen guitarist Jon Klein and Guildhall Conservatory graduate, cellist, accordionist, and multi-instrumentalist Martin McCarrick. For the first time in their decade-long career, Siouxsie and the Banshees were a five-piece and with this lineup, they would write their most commercially successful, most cinematic record yet.

You may have already guessed the central thesis of this book, which is that we can better understand Siouxsie and the Banshees' *Peepshow* when we contextualize the album within film and film music studies as opposed to popular music studies. The intention of this book is, therefore, to elucidate the filmic qualities of *Peepshow* through a largely contextual and analytical method with reference to films and film/film music theory. This reading of *Peepshow* takes an interpretive, semiological approach, as opposed to focusing on formalist musical structures. Or, to refer to film theory, the intention is to illuminate the record as filmic, by examining what Barbara Creed called "the interplay of the codes at work"[21] to include matters like narrative structure, dialogue, and editing. In revealing *Peepshow*'s filmic qualities, this book is therefore focused on a number of key areas:

a. Historical and aesthetical film/film music influence on *Peepshow*'s concepts;

b. Genre film and patterns present in the musical and lyrical components;

c. The staging of protagonists and (atypical) narrative structures;

d. Film music, orchestration, form, and the construction of sonic environments.

Conceptual framework

Steven Severin once described *Peepshow* as "more a concept than a collection of songs."[22] While this book does not theorize *Peepshow* as a concept album, one could say the overarching theme is voyeurism—a subject traceable throughout the band's repertoire.[23] In 1988, Sioux described *Peepshow* to journalist Ronnie Randall:

Each song represents a sort of Peeping Tom situation, with us peering in on each scenario, most of which take place between two people. It's like stripping away the side of an apartment building and watching the different lives going on in parallel in each room/box. We've stripped away the barriers and spied on the secret happenings.[24]

Here, Sioux explicitly references two voyeurism-themed films. First, Michael Powell's deeply controversial (in some countries, censored) *Peeping Tom* (1960) about obsessive amateur filmmaker Mark Lewis and his preying on prostitutes. But this "stripping away of the apartment building"[25] Sioux talks about is not the viewpoint of Mark Lewis in *Peeping Tom*, but the perspective of Jeff Jeffries throughout the entirety of Hitchcock's *Rear Window* (1954) as he spies on his neighbors. Later in 1988, French journalist Jean Daniel Beauvallett suggested that the album title—*Peepshow*—was "unexpected" from the band. Sioux responded, "Yet this was the only way to invite everyone to come and have a look at our own universe."[26] These two descriptions are critical to our understanding of the record since they suggest both the projection and invitation of voyeurism and, as film theorist Laura Mulvey recognized, such a concept is inherent to the pleasure mechanism in cinema.

> The cinema offers a number of possible pleasures. One is scopophilia. There are circumstances in which looking itself is a source of pleasure, just as, in the reverse formation, there is pleasure in being looked at.[27]

Let's now consider how *Peepshow* was first presented to the music industry. Polydor's *Peepshow* press release featured a band image, as well as a close-up shot of Sioux's eye, situating seeing, watching—perhaps even the *female gaze* to flip the Mulvian term[28]—as *Peepshow*'s central thematic. This single, striking image is one that features throughout some of the band's most cited film influences: Roman Polanski's close-up shot of lead protagonist Carol's eye as the opening credits roll at the beginning of his shock thriller *Repulsion* (1965); Marion's lifeless eye as she lay dead in the bath having just been murdered by Norman Bates in Alfred Hitchcock's *Psycho* (1960); and the Buñuelian eye so violently sliced open at the beginning of *Un Chien Andalou* (1929). These three films can all be considered *paracinematic*, that is, they do not conform to conventional cinematic form or narrative. Instead, paracinema features atypical narratives, disruptions to temporal flow, a focus on psychological topics coupled with non-traditional musical scores—features also present in the tracks on *Peepshow*. In *Peepshow*, however, we hear the band drawing upon a much broader paracinematic source base than European art house.

Siouxsie and the Banshees' love of horror B movies, particularly those made by Hammer and AIP, is well-documented. Sioux in particular spoke highly of Roger Corman's Edgar Allan Poe adaptations, including *The Masque of the Red Death* (1964) and *The Pit and the Pendulum* (1961), and the sense of unpretentious, tongue-in-cheek pantomime camp such films portrayed, albeit through an unconvincing horror lens. This facet of cinema, with its cheesy, predictable narratives, wooden acting, and low budget aesthetics may seem a world away from the sophisticated art house classics of Polanski and his ilk, but there are many similarities. They, too, can be considered paracinematic. Hammer and AIP B movies and the "trash aesthetics" of low culture often conflate with European art cinema because they both oppose cinema's traditional production values[29] in terms of narrative structures, protagonists, settings, and storyworlds. Both Horror B movies and European art cinema often "handle explosive social material that mainstream cinema is reluctant to touch"[30] and as such, create alternative, cult cinemas that exist in parallel to Hollywood. As Mark Janovich suggested, "Roger Corman was a heroic outsider who refused the standards of mainstream film and courted imperfection."[31]

That Siouxsie and the Banshees identified with Corman and the wider paracinematic world makes perfect sense. The band had often referred to themselves as "non-musicians"[32] opposed to one-dimensional music,[33] as outsiders who avoided cliques[34] and trends,[35] as unpredictable and iconoclastic.[36] Paradoxically, however, the band asserted themselves as "pop,"[37] were signed to a major label both in the United Kingdom and in the United States, and by 1988 had amassed eight hit albums and more than a dozen hit singles.[38] This contradiction, this refusal to participate in—or draw influence from—the popular cultural mainstream, yet simultaneously demand a place in it, was at the very core of Siouxsie and the Banshees' aesthetic, as Irene Morra noted, they "redefined traditional assumptions of communal expression" and "signaled a refusal to acknowledge the established convention."[39]

Siouxsie and the Banshees are to popular music what paracinema is to Hollywood: a sideshow to the mainstream. But from where in this paracinematic world does the peep show situ derive? On a literal level, *Peepshow*'s namesake is found in British director Ken Russell's first unfunded attempt at short silent filmmaking. Russell's *Peepshow* (1956) is a homage to a cinematic style called Weimar expressionism; with its black and white *vignette* and vaudeville inspired storyline featuring a somnambulist routine, it draws heavily on silent film aesthetics. Russell's peep show is, however, a pop-up tent featuring a comedy act with a life-sized doll; Siouxsie and the Banshees' peep show, however, resembles more contemporary, grittier depictions.

The site of the peep show as depicted on film is a powerful one, a code that conjures up images of the criminal underworld, censorship, social deterioration, and decay and loss of self-control. This is used for dramatic effect in Frank Capra's *It's A Wonderful Life* (1946), where the alternate reality of *Pottersville* features a seedy, run down district complete with casinos and a peep show prominently featured on the town's main strip. A later example is found in Francis Ford Coppola's *Rumble Fish* (1983) a stark, black and white contemporary noir; its downtown, gangland *mise en scène* features a seedy strip full of drug dealers, prostitutes, and gangs, and a prominent peep show. Perhaps the most relevant example can be found in Martin Scorsese's seminal *Taxi Driver* (1976), in which the "Show & Tell" X-rated cinema and peep show becomes the site of lead protagonist Travis Bickle's pleasure *and* disgust. Throughout the film, we see Bickle's evolving infatuation with the peep show setting as he detaches further from reality, at one point taking his love interest, Betsy, on a date to "Show and Tell." The extraordinary disconnect between both the film audience and Betsy's rationality and Travis's irrational mind is portrayed to stunning effect via Scorcese's direction, but more so in the final—and arguably one of the best—scores by Bernard Herrmann. Throughout the film, Herrmann uses a creeping, foreboding, dynamically ascending string-led phrase to highlight Travis's anxiety and the rising intensity of his anger. Later, Herrmann uses a descending bass/cello motif to underscore Travis's perspective of New York as a site of moral decay. That Herrmann contrasts this with interpolating downtown, clubby jazz numbers perfectly illustrates the reality of New York club life and the irrationality and contradictions playing out in Travis's mind. On *Peepshow*, we hear this Herrmannian style play out, particularly in opening track "Peek-A-Boo" where a largely avant-garde inspired, radiophonic underscore features chorus interpolations of Warren and Mercer's jazz standard "Jeepers Creepers."[40]

Peepshow was mixed at the Marquee Studios in the heart of London's Soho. This locality, a queer district synonymous with sex shops, fetish clubs, and, of course, peep shows, consolidated the album not just musically but thematically and aesthetically. In the mid-1980s, the Soho peep show was enjoying a renaissance; in one famous case, workers took over an establishment as a cooperative

> Eight booths surround a narrow stage and for a bare 50p customers get a scanty 1 minute 40 seconds peeping through a glazed slot as the naked ladies dance to music. When the time runs out, a shutter comes down.[41]

During *Peepshow*'s mix process, Siouxsie and the Banshees managed to bottle Soho's seedy nighttime atmosphere and liberally apply it to the entire record. This is particularly apparent in "Catwalk" (a "Peek-A-Boo" B-side), the inspiration for which Sioux explained:

> Marquee Studios was accessed via an old dark alleyway. Every night, long after midnight with great ceremony and commotion, a "lady of the night" on her way home from "work" would stop to feed the starving local felines who would miraculously appear from out of the shadows on time.[42]

Peepshow exemplifies Siouxsie and the Banshees' ability to convey such powerfully evocative visuals via music. Contextually, this is a record that delivers a largely paracinematic aesthetic via—as will become clear later on—the most musically and technically accomplished songs Siouxsie and the Banshees ever put to record. Sioux herself cited *Peepshow* as her "favorite"[43] Banshees record, as well as "our best album. Full stop."[44]

In *Peepshow*'s press release, Severin stated "For the first time . . . we've done an album with a black and white structure and allow the listener to color the edges."[45] This might be an allusion to silent era cinema, references to which feature heavily throughout *Peepshow*, but the album is not an instrumental record—its lyrics are as complex, poetic, and equally rich as its musical elements. Neither is silent film the only historical film chapter referenced in *Peepshow*. This record takes us on a journey through film and film music history, the album tracks also exemplifying film genre. To that end, *Peepshow* is considered in this book as Siouxsie and the Banshees' own *film maudit*,[46] (a collection of-largely cursed and overlooked-films), for *Peepshow* is a heavily intertextual record reflecting a bricolage of mostly paracinematic film influence.

Genre film

This book situates each song within a cinematic genre context with plenty of references to films, allowing us to trace particular aesthetic patterns in the music and draw parallels to such patterns found in film. Genre films are usually built around specific frameworks, as Rick Altman stated,

> constantly opposing cultural values to counter-cultural values, genre films regularly depend on dual protagonists and dualistic structures (producing what I have called dual-focus texts).[47]

Altman recognized how genre films rely upon the notion of duality, in terms of opposing—and sometimes conflicting—protagonist characters and agendas, narratives, and values. This notion of genre film duality is foregrounded in *Peepshow* in a multitude of ways: its orchestration and electric/acoustic, popular/classical, live/recorded dualities present in the instrumentation; the dualistic staging of protagonists including the stripper/her audience in "Peek-A-Boo," the frightened young girl/the monster in "Rawhead and Bloodybones," two lovers covered in ornaments of gold and/or positioned on a grand, war-torn stage in "The Last Beat of My Heart," Sioux/Dmitri Shostakovich in "Rhapsody"; the dualities of texture from Glassian minimalism in "Carousel" to the densely textured, operatic "Rhapsody." Like many musically complex records, *Peepshow* is full of angular and oblique, yet smooth and formalist contradictions in melody, in arrangement, and in lyrics. A major duality is the peep show environment itself, for the album—just like Scorcese's "Show & Tell" in *Taxi Driver*—is simultaneously a participation in voyeuristic behavior and a critique of it.

So how are *Peepshow*'s album tracks organized into this book's film genre framework? Opening track and lead single "Peek-A-Boo" is situated in the context of early cinema and deals with Weimar-era film. The Second single "The Killing Jar" is analyzed in the context of the noir (albeit a postmodern, Lynchian noir) crime thriller genre and its lyrical resemblance to William Wyler's adaptation of John Fowles's 1963 novel *The Collector*. Album track "Scarecrow" bears all the hallmarks of musical film, while lyrically alluding to *The Wizard of Oz* (1939), *The Wicker Man* (1973) as well as Dennis Potter's 1980s teleplay *The Singing Detective* (1986). "Carousel," with its fairground setting complete with found sounds and a synthesized calliope, evokes early twentieth-century travelling vaudeville, while also explicitly referencing Tobe Hooper's 1981 horror *The Fun House*, as well as merry-go-rounds featured prominently in *The Twilight Zone*, Jack Clayton's 1983 Disney adaptation of Ray Bradbury's novel *Something Wicked This Way Comes*, and, of course, Hitchcock's *Strangers on a Train*.

Trains and the spectacular visuals of speed and collision are one of cinema's earliest tropes dating back to Edison, and the later realization of the powerful motif of the railroad in Western genre is musically depicted in "Burn-Up," a classic homage to both Sergio Leone and Ennio Morricone. "Ornaments of Gold" and "Turn to Stone" musically epitomize Siouxsie and the Banshees at their escapist peak. The fantastical conflation of mythologies, theologies, folklore, and film influence create two of *Peepshow*'s most otherworldly tracks. References to *Cleopatra* (1963) and *Eureka* (1983) with passages from the Koran in "Ornaments of Gold" are augmented with a quasi-Eastern (hammered) dulcimer melody, whereas the reference to "the sickle moon" in "Turn to Stone" places them both in the Islamic world. The petrification theme in

"Turn To Stone" is grounded in Greek mythology and the Medusa, yet also features widely in fantasy and sci-fi film and literature, for example, in Fritz Lang's *Metropolis* (1927) and in C. S. Lewis's literary classic *The Lion, The Witch and the Wardrobe* (1950). "Rawhead and Bloodybones" synergizes classic British and US folklore with aspects of voice metamorphosis, "monster" protagonists, and environmental tropes common to horror film genre. And finally, "The Last Beat of My Heart" and "Rhapsody" are taken together as *Peepshow*'s epic encore. Both staged in war-torn *mise en scène* complete with vast soundscapes and grand *libretti*, "The Last Beat of My Heart" features elements of melodrama and spectacle in mid-twentieth-century epic, whereas the Soviet Union "Rhapsody" setting features allusions to proto-epics including Sergei Eisenstein's *The Battleship Potemkin* (1925) and Mikheil Chiaureli's *The Fall of Berlin* (1950).

Protagonists and (atypical) narrative structures

Siouxsie and the Banshees' collection title, *Once Upon a Time: The Singles* (1981), perfectly frames their song-as-story, literary approach to writing. Like much of the band's repertoire, *Peepshow*'s songwriting credits are attributed to either Sioux ("Peek-A-Boo," "Carousel," "Burn-Up," "Ornaments of Gold," "Rawhead and Bloodybones") or Severin ("The Killing Jar," "Scarecrow," "Turn To Stone," "Rhapsody") or to them both ("The Last Beat of My Heart"). Their songwriting method, particularly on *Peepshow*, demonstrates a commitment to creating a storyworld within the song's structure. Severin, a self-proclaimed "anti-personal writer"[48] suggested,

> We aimed to create, in four or five minutes, some other place you could go to create a setting without (myself or Siouxsie) actually taking on a role in that world. By that I mean that Siouxsie didn't make herself a central character in that imaginary landscape. When I was writing lyrics, I was aware of not creating a character for her to inhabit, and the same applies to her own lyrics.[49]

Severin repeatedly cited literary influences on his creation of lyrical storyworlds. For example, he said of "Scarecrow" "[Angela] Carter's The Bloody Chamber made me want to write it as a modern fairy tale"[50] and of "The Last Beat of My Heart," "I'd been reading a lot of Russian poets who were banned during that time."[51] What we hear throughout *Peepshow* is the manifestation of a filmic—and to a lesser degree, literary—approach to character formation in song. Severin speaks of constructing *mise en scène*, the aesthetics of escapism and the situating of protagonists within beautifully defined settings. Lyrics are scarcely sung from first-person perspective and rarely attempt first-person emotive expression, as Sioux stated: "I don't want lyrics to become an indulgent confessional. I use 'he' or 'she' instead, 'I' just reduces everything to indulgence."[52]

Each of *Peepshow*'s songs play out in an evocative cinematic storyworld: each has an environment, setting or "stage," and every song features strong leading and secondary protagonists. These characters negotiate various encounters, trials, and tribulations and, in most instances, there is a conclusion. In saying that, *Peepshow*'s song attributes feature just as many contradictions and resistances to the narrative flow. For example, while the "once upon a time" introduction is always present, we never hear a "happily ever after" resolution. In the finale of "Peek-A-Boo," Sioux's stripper is left alone on the peep show stage, getting up from all fours and crying bitterly; are the fairground attendees still aboard the "Carousel," or are we listening to a dream sequence?; and, in the ultimate cliffhanger, are the lovers ever reunited in "The Last Beat of My Heart"? In two songs—"The Killing Jar" and "Rawhead and Bloodybones"—(at least one of) the featured protagonist(s) dies a tortured death, while a flipside of that is heard in "Rhapsody" where the lead protagonist describes the horrors of genocide from an apparent, staged distance.

The protagonists—and the interactions between them—are also unconventional. "Burn-Up" relies upon pyromaniacal King Salamander to carry the story alone. And in "Scarecrow," Sioux's young girl protagonist interacts with a (imaginary?) friend creating a similar character duality to Dorothy and The Scarecrow in Victor Fleming's *The Wizard of Oz* (1939). Sioux stated, "I like someone to be a good narrator, to tell a story in song."[53] Yet in most of *Peepshow*'s songs, the narrative flow is nonlinear, disrupted and confused. *Peepshow*'s songs—as they are organized in the album's large-scale form as well as the micro aspects of individual song arrangements—apparently jump between historical eras, seasons, and past, present, and future narrative tenses. "Scarecrow," for example, begins set in summer. The outdoors environment complete with crickets buzzing in heat soaked grasses lends the first verse a balmy summer night setting, yet by the second verse, the glockenspiel leitmotif signifies Jack Frost, a mainstay of historical winter folklore. There are many other ways in which *Peepshow* negotiates time: the conflation of backward and forward orchestration in "Peek-A-Boo," the lyrical references to memory in "Carousel," the staccato, backward vocal samples in "Turn to Stone," the wartime stages of "The Last Beat of My Heart," and "Rhapsody" among many other examples lends the entire record an overall sense of Buñuelian/Dalían temporal disorder. We are never quite sure where—or *when*—we are. And the construction of this temporal maze featuring unpredictable twists, turns, circles, and dead ends is intended, focused, and realized. Like in the majority of Siouxsie and the Banshees' work, the overarching influence of Carroll's nonsensical *Alice's Adventures in Wonderland* (1865) is clearly heard.

Narratively, *Peepshow* does not draw from conventional Hollywood cinematic structures and predictable boy-meets-girl love stories with concomitant emotion-oriented story lines. In *Film: A Critical Introduction*, Pramaggiore and Wallis outline the conventions of narrative structure: the sequences of events and systematic presentation in the definition of narrative film.[54] They posit aspects of clarity, unity, clearly defined characters with understandable motivations, and definitive closure as the principle "rules" of Hollywood film. Conversely, they suggest the unconventional as broken chronology, "muddy" characters with dubious or unclear motivations, a lack of closure and general unreliability.[55] It would be easy to argue *Peepshow* as a classic example of the narrative unconventionality Pramaggiore and Wallis theorize, yet Siouxsie and the Banshees occasionally contradict their *film maudit* with sporadic ascription to Hollywood convention. For example, the "long lost love" is quite possibly the single most popular trope in Hollywood cinema and is clearly drawn upon in "The Last Beat of My Heart" and "Burn-Up" clearly emulates the Western, a quintessential twentieth-century American film genre.

So on the one hand, *Peepshow* can be read as exemplifying the kind of cinema that ruptures tradition: the nonsensical abstraction of Dada; the unpredictable and synchronically disoriented confusion invoked by Buñuelian/Dalían surrealism; the topsy-turvy studio constructivism of Weimar expressionism; the brutal, explicit violence of the 1970s Scorsese/Ford Coppola canon; the sense of disconcerting unease embodied in British occult horror; and the dualities and distortion in industrial Lynchian noir. On the other hand, *Peepshow* is a nod and a wink, an occasional tongue-in-cheek parody of the pomp and grandiosity of Hollywood: of Selznick's opulent epics; Kubrick's academy defying auteurism; Leone/Morricone's iconic Westerns; the recurrent Wagnerian *leitmotifs* used to denote the presence of protagonists; and the foregrounding of Martin McCarrick's cello as symbolizing romanticism—the clichéd underscore of Hollywood's golden age.

That this book focuses on film is *not* to say that Siouxsie and the Banshees were not inspired by music—the influence of David Bowie, Roxy Music, The Velvet Underground, and the minimalist canon on the group is well-documented. Parallels between the music in *Peepshow* and that of other artists, particularly Bowie, can certainly be drawn, but this book aims to tell a different story. As early as 1978, Siouxsie and the Banshees said, "We don't see ourselves in the same context as rock 'n' roll groups"[56] yet this critical statement—like so much of the band's interview material—somehow failed to sink in. That the press insisted on contextualizing Siouxsie and the Banshees in scenes and genres they were never part of led to the band being one of the most misunderstood, misreceived, and understudied artists in popular music history. In this book, therefore, my intention is to see if framing the band in a film context (and not in "rock 'n' roll") helps address that issue.

Film music, orchestration, form, and the sonic environment

That Siouxsie and the Banshees drew inspiration from Hitchcock's iconic noir thrillers is well known, but to focus on this aspect exclusively would exclude the depth of their influence; as Sioux stated, "While we love . . . putting a sort of Hitchcockian edge to our music it's led to a lot of misconceptions."[57] This misinterpretation, I would argue, stems from the Banshees being (a) inspired by a much broader film base than simply those made by Hitchcock and (b) less influenced by Hitchcock and more by the music of his long time composer Bernard Herrmann.

Herrmann was a maverick. As a "master of diverse instrumentation,"[58] he defied Hollywood's sentimental over-reliance on romantic string underscoring with jagged and discordant phrasing, the use of delicate, upper register percussion to invoke spine-tingling effects and exploited the potential of recording processes to (unnaturally) foreground quieter orchestral instruments. David Butler described Herrmann's style as

> rejection of extended, melodic lines; emphasis on instrumental and harmonic color; distinctive groupings of instruments as opposed to reliance on the large scale orchestra; a predilection for small musical "cells" and the use of the ostinato device in particular.[59]

Unlike prior Hollywood film music, Herrmann's compositions were powerful filmic mechanisms, the kind of scores Royal Brown called "dramatically motivated"[60] as opposed to those that evoked "the period in which the films were made"[61] or that which is "wallpaper soporific."[62] Songwriters Sioux and Severin were drawn to such scores that not only equaled commonly foregrounded elements of narrative and *mise en scène*, but those that rendered such aspects secondary. Examples of these kinds of films include Norm Ferguson's *Fantasia* (1940), about which Claudia Gorban suggested "subordinate(s) cinematic/narrative logic to musical logic"[63] and Hitchcock's *Vertigo* (1958), of which Jack Sullivan said that "it is hard to think of any movie more dependent upon the seductiveness of its score."[64] Unsurprisingly, then, extracts from both these film scores appeared on Sioux and Severin's 2014 Mojo cover compilation *It's a Wonderfull Life*.[65]

Nino Rota is another composer whose work had an everlasting effect on Severin, who described Rota's score for Fellini's *Casanova* (1976) as a "masterpiece."[66] Rota's signature manifested in his ability to apply diverse orchestration from celesta through acoustic guitar, electric keyboard to flute equally across heavily textured, yet unpredictable scoring. Building on Herrmann's modernist approach to film score, Rota's application of an even broader based instrumental palette dramatically expanded the filmic dimensions of narrative and *mise en scène* like never before. Rota has been described as "a musician for whom there existed no barriers of genres, categories or qualifications."[67] And the influence of both Herrmann and Rota on Siouxsie and the Banshees manifests more in *Peepshow* than in any other record they made. We hear this through the breadth of orchestration, the use of delicate orchestral instruments as *leitmotifs*—consider the chimes attached to the owner of the submerged glass hand in "The Killing Jar" or the glockenspiel motif for Jack Frost in "Scarecrow"—and the manipulation of temporal elements to portray psychological aspects of urgency, fear, foreboding, and anxiety. These musical gestures are drawn from film and *not* popular music.

Another of *Peepshow*'s major accomplishments is its large-scale form; the way these songs seamlessly traverse classical romanticism, modernism, and minimalism; radiophonics, the avant-garde, and art rock; jazz, reggae, and folk; even bluegrass, flamenco, and polka is unparalleled, not only in Siouxsie and the Banshees' repertoire but in wider popular music of the era.

Contrasts can be drawn between this multi-genre approach and the ways music was constructed in modular form for turn of the twentieth-century "photoplays"—silent films that required a broad range of musical accompaniment, as Müller and Plebuch noted of F. W. Murnau's Weimar classic *Nosferatu* (1922),

> Five instrumental movements . . . . Together they form a little catalog of musico-dramatic topoi ranging from pastoral, folk dance, and hunt to funeral march, misterioso, storm scenes, ghosts, and goblins evocative of the nocturnal and supernatural images of dark romanticism. Every piece is defined in character and offers a range of possible thematic associations.[68]

Yet *Peepshow*'s Weimar aesthetic draws from cabaret as well as photoplay; we hear the influence of German composer Freidrich Hollaender[69] ingrained in the record. His classic, jazzy club numbers including "Ich bin von Kopf bis Fuß auf Liebe eingestellt"[70] and "Ich bin die fesche Lola"[71] both from Josef von Sternberg's *The Blue Angel* (1930) lent Marlene Dietrich the perfect vehicle to drive the allure of her captivating protagonist Lola Lola. We hear a clear allusion to Hollaender's "show time" standards in the introduction to "Peek-A-Boo" with its dramatic string motifs and stage-stomping kick drum. But Hollaender's influence runs much deeper. *Peepshow*'s quick-fire positioning of back-to-back genre contrasts has a direct parallel to Hollaender's Academy award-winning score for Roy Rowland's adaptation of Dr. Seuss's *The 5000 Fingers of Dr. T* (1953)—a film cited by both Sioux and Budgie as influential to their work.[72] This dark, surrealist film focuses on a little boy who, tired of his strict piano practice routine, dozes off and dreams of his tyrannical teacher—Dr. Terwilliker—who has devised a one-thousand-octave mega piano to be played by 5000 fingers of little boys, while casting every other musician and instrument to his dungeon. With its exhaustive race through tango, cabaret, and flamenco, Hollander's "The Hypnotic Duel" epitomizes the composer's multi-genre inspired score. Similarly, *Peepshow* is a whirlwind tour through contrasting (film) music styles.

The 5000 Fingers . . . features another key piece titled "The Dungeon Ballet," a stunning montage showcasing all instruments of the orchestra as they take on a surrealist twist, in both a statement on the versatility of orchestral instruments beyond classical music and to critique the focus on piano in classical music pedagogy. *Peepshow* is, of course, equally instrumentally diverse: the album foregrounds McCarrick's cello, as well as Budgie's tuned and untuned percussion as it traverses dense, tribal Taiko-inspired rhythmic textures through Glassian and Reichian minimalism: everything from timpani to Güiro, triangle to vibraphone, chimes to temple blocks is heard on this record. Synthesized brass and woodwinds, a harmonica, a hammered dulcimer—even a synthesized *calliope*—contrast Jon Klein's metamorphic guitar, most of the time so distorted, modulated, or otherwise camouflaged that it only occasionally resembles a guitar. Meanwhile, Severin's often chorus-laden bass guitar circles around each song as if surveilling the entire proceedings. This instrumentation twists and turns throughout *Peepshow* in a surrealist orchestration mirroring Hollaender's score. But there are two further significant parallels to be drawn: first, one instrument that does not feature anywhere on *Peepshow* is piano—the only instrument excluded from Dr. Terwilliker's dungeon. And secondly, the instrument that apparently interrupts the orchestral score in Hollaender's

"Dungeon Ballet" is the accordion, which is the foregrounded instrument on two of *Peepshow*'s three singles: "Peek-A-Boo" and "The Last Beat of My Heart."

The analytical detail in this book focuses on narratives and orchestration but also on the construction of sonic environments befitting both the lyrical and musical elements. Sioux herself was always focused on "trying to create an atmosphere: how a sound resonates and makes an effect"[73] and suggested the creation of atmosphere had "always been very important"[74] to her. In *Peepshow*, we hear multiple soundscapes; the inside of the peep show arena in "Peek-A-Boo" and the outdoor fairground and calliope in "Carousel" are just two examples of what composer R. Murray Schafer referred to as

> the sonic environment. The term may refer to actual environments, or to abstract constructions such as musical compositions and tape montages, particularly when considered as an environment.[75]

Schafer's composition philosophy includes environmental sounds as equal to musical sounds—an outlook undoubtedly shared by Siouxsie and the Banshees. In *Peepshow*, we hear these environmental sounds—both found and constructed—in specific contexts, as Schafer's fellow composer and colleague Barry Truax noted,

> in the soundscape composition . . . it is precisely the environmental context that is preserved, enhanced and exploited by the composer. The listener's past experience, associations, and patterns of soundscape perception are

called upon by the composer and thereby integrated within the compositional strategy. Part of the composer's intent may also be to enhance the listener's awareness of environmental sound.[76]

Here, these matters are construed from *Peepshow*'s production, which in this case—where the intention is to elucidate the evocative, visual, filmic aspects of the music—is more useful than focusing exclusively on lyrics, poetic devices and diegeses, or on formalist musical structures, as Alan Williams suggested

> that in sound recording, as in image recording, the apparatus performs a significant perceptual work *for us*—isolating, intensifying, *analyzing* sonic and visual material. It gives an implied physical perspective on image or sound source, though not the full, material context of everyday vision or hearing, but *the signs of* such a physical situation.[77]

This book, therefore, examines the temporal, dynamic, and spatial attributes of the songs in order to elucidate *Peepshow*'s many storyworlds, those being combined narratives and environments. What is clear from analyzing *Peepshow* is that such sonic aesthetics form definite sonic stages, sound atmospheres largely constructed through production techniques. These stages situate the protagonists accurately in relation to what we envision from the music and lyrical narratives. Let's take each track in turn and see how *Peepshow* may be read as a filmic record.

*   *   *

Early Cinema

[LULU] I won't be sold. That's worse than prison.
— *Pandora's Box*

[SOLDIER] What about Péman?
[PÉMAN] I'm done for.
[SOLDIER] So are we, but we're going.
[PÉMAN] Yes, but you've got accordions, hippopotamuses,
wrenches, mountain goats and . . .
— *L'Age D'Or*

With its Weimar aesthetic, top hat, and accordion, "Peek-A-Boo" is *Peepshow*'s dramatic exposition. Encompassing a voyeuristic theme and narrated from a seedy underworld, both its composition and storyworld are steeped in cinematic reference, particularly that of 1920s Weimar Germany. In *Silent Cinema*, Brian Robb noted that this "30-year period from the end of the nineteenth century through to the coming of sound in 1929 saw dramatic technological and aesthetic change in the cinematic arts."[1] Featuring extraordinary orchestration and arrangement, it is toward the end of this critical thirty-year period in early cinema that "Peek-A-Boo" so vividly evokes; an era prone to censorship as directors became more confident of projecting the "dark side" via cinema.[2] In 1989, Steven Severin said,

> It [*Peepshow*] all sort of started with as we were doing the album we were referring to this book a lot which was called *The Archaeology of the Cinema*, which I had found in a second hand shop in London, and it was concerned with very early devices that made moving pictures, starting as far back as with things like the Camera Obscura and Kaleidoscopes and such.[3]

This fascination with mechanical, pre-projector cinematic devices, Edison's kinetoscope, and, much earlier still, eighteenth and nineteenth-century peep shows, is clearly embodied in "Peek-A-Boo." Interestingly enough, as Erkki Huhtamo stated in *The Pleasures of the Peephole*, the eroticization of peep shows developed in the twentieth century, whereas before then the peep show "was essentially a virtual voyaging medium, providing the peepers opportunities to 'visit' locations and events that most people could not have witnessed in situ during their entire lifetimes."[4] In the book *The Archaeology of the Cinema* that Severin referenced, author C. W. Ceram also stated that

> Peep shows were among the commonest entertainments of the street and fairground throughout the 18th and 19th Centuries. The showman would let down successive scenes by means of the strings at the side, usually sensational episodes from contemporary life, accompanying the display with a lively commentary.[5]

Ceram also noted that many peep shows featured perspective views, often set up as board panels inside the peep show device. The mechanism of these primitive devices often resulted in a warped picture due to position of pictures in the frame, which, paired with poor candle lighting, would sometimes create distorted views. These twisted scenes evoke another key filmic influence on *Peepshow*: that of Robert Weine's benchmark expressionist film *Das Cabinet des Dr Caligari* (1920).[6] Weine's classic film signified the beginning of *Caligarisme*, films and artwork featuring distorted time frames and scenes, twisted orchestration, dream-like atmospheres, and dark, proto-noir themes.[7] "Peek-A-Boo"—like the entirety of *Peepshow*—is a good example of *Caligarisme*; as it creeps up back stairs and slinks into dark stalls, the track immediately evokes the stark, Escher-esque silhouettes so intrinsic to *Caligari*. Yet the *Caligarisme* in "Peek-A-Boo" is sonically as well as aesthetically embodied, for the painstaking coordination of *mise en scène* in Weine's *Das Cabinet des Dr Caligari* was a benchmark in "studio constructivism." This term was coined by Paul Rotha and refers to the meticulously detailed process of building a film in a studio, which characterizes "that curious air of completeness, of finality, that surrounds each product of the German studios."[8] A parallel can be drawn between such studio constructivism and "Peek-A-Boo"; with its tape-based composition and multi-intertextual form,[9] the track is a patchwork sonic tessellation, as Budgie stated, "There are no metronomical sounds, its simply the way we've put it together that makes it sound so concise."[10]

While "Peek-A-Boo"'s *Caligarisme* sonic arrangement and visual imaginary is integral to its function, its lead protagonist—Sioux's pathos-soaked stripper—is drawn from another pillar of Weimar cinema. At the very heart of Weimar culture was the "New Woman"; a sexually empowered, fiercely courageous, and independent female epitomized by Marlene Dietrich's Lola Lola in *The Blue Angel* (1930). In her commanding performance of the definitive Weimar flapper, Dietrich's cabaret androgyneity challenged female stereotypes and redefined depictions of on-screen sexuality more than forty years prior to Liza Minnelli in Bob Fosse's Weimar homage *Cabaret* (1972). Sioux's top-hatted *Peepshow* persona as printed in the record sleeve is a definitive nod to Dietrich's Lola Lola—a cabaret star—but the stripper protagonist in "Peek-A-Boo" is an oppressed, yet paradoxically more forceful incarnation of the Weimar flapper. The heroine of "Peek-A-Boo" bears more resemblance to Louise Brooks, specifically Lulu in *Pandora's Box* (1929) and Thymian in *Diary of a Lost Girl* (1929), as both characters exude prominent yet ambiguous sexuality while simultaneously projecting feelings of rebellion and disgust. "Peek-A-Boo"'s sense of sexual entrapment in the seedy peep show is exactly the aesthetic captured by *Strassenfilme*: a type of Weimar "New Objectivity"—*die neue Sachlichkeit*—social realist film[11] depicting "sordid and commonplace stories of social crisis, disintegration, starvation and prostitution."[12] The cold and overcrowded reformatory where poor Thymian is holed up under the watch of domineering matron (Valeska Gert) in *Diary of a Lost Girl* and the damp basement where Lulu and Alwa face poverty and starvation at the bleak conclusion of *Pandora's Box*—and the prostitution narratives surrounding both—epitomize the aesthetics of *Strassenfilme* that "Peek-A-Boo" so convincingly evokes.

While lyrically, lead single "Peek-A-Boo" situates Sioux's stripper protagonist well and truly at the center of a twentieth-century peep show stage, musically, the song resembles the clunky, mechanical contraptions featured in Ceram's *Archaeology of the Cinema*. To that end, "Peek-A-Boo" embodies *both* meanings of the peep show as the site of both eroticism and escapism. Sioux's stripper relates the dank stench of the claustrophobic peep show's twisted interior so evocatively, we are transported to 1920s Berlin regardless of its more contemporary Soho locality.[13]

Musically complex and widely received as Siouxsie and the Banshees' most accomplished single,[14] "Peek-A-Boo" is a good example of multi-intertextual form. First, the backward drum loop and brass that underpins it is a sample drawn from "Gun" (1987), a John Cale cover that featured on the Banshees' previous album *Through the Looking Glass* (1987). For this retrograde rhythmic foundation to work once consolidated with further, performed instruments, recordist Mike Hedges undertook a constructivist process of splicing tiny segments of tape to achieve a consistent tempo, since when played backwards, "Gun" was slowing down.

> It [Gun] was all on two-inch analogue tape, so I actually physically edited it, taking out slivers of tape as it slowed down. I'd take out a sixteenth of an inch to speed up a particular beat, and as it got slower I'd be taking out a quarter or even half an inch of tape to pull it all up to the same speed. I then copied that tape across to another multi-track and that was the basis of the new song, in tempo and backwards.[15]

In the late 1980s, an era dominated by digital sampling and sequencing, these techniques were anachronistic in popular music, moreover they resembled the innovative tape composition techniques of the BBC's radiophonic workshop, where sound designers Delia Derbyshire, Daphne Oram, and Desmond Briscoe created soundscapes made from found sounds, synthesis, and tape effects. These compositions were not intended for commercial release, but instead as television and radio play theme tunes, as well as the underscoring of radio serials. Their effects-based compositional techniques had more in common with film music than with commercial recordings. Sioux was—is—a big fan of this small electronic studio, as she said, "The sounds, the noises, the theremins. I love it!"[16] And Severin cited tape recording as his first foray into composition, "The first thing I ever got involved with was playing with tape recorders, making loops."[17] That these techniques were employed on "Peek-A-Boo" makes perfect sense. While the foregrounded sample-collage techniques resulted in the track sometimes being interpreted as hip hop,[18] it is more the case that hip hop's sample-collage aesthetics is a late twentieth-century style of *music concréte*, which André Hodeir described as

> recording various sounds (either musical sounds or noises of indeterminate pitch) and then, by speeding them up, slowing them down, filtering or inverting them, metamorphose these sounds into "sound objects."[19]

"Peek-A-Boo," therefore, is fundamentally a musique concréte composition. The result is an aural illusion of a repetitive, mechanical loop: the conflation of retrograde sample and Budgie's forward kick and snare manifest in an apparent "locked groove," the circular, rhythmic equivalent of a revolving zoetrope.

Secondly, the chorus in "Peek-A-Boo" features a lyrical quotation modified from the 1938 jazz standard "Jeepers Creepers," written by Warren & Mercer, performed by Louis Armstrong and featured in the film *Going Places* (1938). This conflation of musique concréte and pre-war jazz situates "Peek-A-Boo" in the 1940s, yet its feature instrument— McCarrick's accordion—posits the track both earlier, in turn-of-the-century European polka and vaudeville, *and* later, since it alludes to the prostitution narrative central to Edith Piaf's 1955 traditional classic "L'Accordeoniste."[20] This combination of intertextual historicity and forward/backward orchestration pushes and pulls "Peek-A-Boo" in opposing directions resulting in a surrealist temporality— the sense of strange, nonlinear sequences used by Buñuel

and Dalí in films like *L'Age D'Or* and *Un Chien Andalou*—
that ultimately makes the track difficult to *place*, or as
Todd Nakamine wrote, "totally un-pigeonhole-able."[21] Yet
musically, with its combination of radiophonic foundation
and forward-performed instruments, as well as featuring
both acoustic and synthesized orchestration, "Peek-A-Boo"
could be considered a representation of what Rick Altman
identified as a "transitional crisis" between live and recorded
sound, electronic and acoustic instrumentation during 1920s
and 1930s silent cinema.[22] And it is right there, at the height of
Weimar cinema, where "Peek-A-Boo" sits most comfortably.

Sioux's addition of the "Peek-A-Boo" chorus hook to
the "Jeepers Creepers" quotation encapsulates three key
thematics: First, in the repeated phrase "peek-a-boo," we
find the concept of *miegakure* from Japanese aesthetics—the
notion of "hide and reveal" originating in shadow plays.[23]
Without digressing too far, it is important to note here both
Sioux and Budgie's love of Japan, Japanese imagery, clothing,
film, and the influence of Taiko on Budgie's drumming.
Sioux's kimono-clad Japanese image adorned Kaleidoscope-
era magazine covers and picture discs,[24] and Japanese film,
particularly Shindo Kaneto's stark, obsessive thriller *Onibaba*
(1964), was regularly cited by Sioux as a key influence.[25]

Secondly, "Peek-A-Boo" explicitly evokes the "peep
show" environment, the stage on which Sioux's objectified
stripper persona performs. And thirdly, the phrase serves to
infantalize the peep show attendees: let's not forget that taken
literally, *peek-a-boo* is a universal game usually played with a
baby. That this infantalization takes place in the sexualized
peep show is what renders "Peek-A-Boo" so disturbing, yet

so unmistakably Siouxsie and the Banshees; "Peek-A-Boo" is at once a projection of disgust, yet simultaneously the embracing and embodiment of it. To top it all off, "Peek-A-Boo" features a dramatic "show time" introduction that again alludes to Hitchcock's *Psycho* with discordant, electronic string stabs reminiscent of Herrmann's iconic shower scene violins.

Earlier, I referred to the "circular" motion of the backward rhythm and brass. This sense of rotation is reinforced by the position of instruments—in particular, the voice—in the stereo field: in "Peek-A-Boo," a performance "stage" is technologically and processually constructed for Sioux's stripper. Severin described an unusual vocal recording where

> Siouxsie recorded her vocal on seven different mikes. One line was recorded on an AKG . . . the muffled vocals you can hear were sung into a "Swedish Slug" which came off an old abandoned tape recorder.[26]

While this explains the timbral differences between each vocal line, the vocal "stage" is constructed through careful organization of each line at different positions in the stereo field. This process would have been done at mix stage, where panning controls on the console would have been used to meticulously place each line. First, alternate lines of each verse vocal are positioned at the center, center right, or center left in the stereo field. The voice, therefore, is continually in motion throughout the song, jumping from one part of the "stage" to another. Additionally, each vocal "set" has been subject to distinctive processing: The vocals positioned center—in verse one, that is lines one, three, and five of eight—are "sung," foregrounded in the mix, close mic'd and, aside from a very short delay, are kept relatively dry with little reverb. Conversely, the vocals positioned center right are delivered harder and, due to their relative position at the rear of mix, appear to be shouted from the back of the "stage." The third set of vocals, those positioned center left, are the most processed of the three. We hear a much weaker voice, one which is distorted and filtered—most probably the "Swedish Slug" set Severin described. The result of the latter filtered effect is, ironically, to "strip" a sound of its high and low frequency content thus leaving its central middle frequency band exposed.[27] This processing accounts for only one of the three thematics described earlier, the construction of the peep show itself—a circular stage upon which the stripper is in continual motion.

The other two thematics—the concept of *miegakure* and the infant game *peek-a-boo* is depicted in the chorus. Here, the lyrical hook "Peek-A-Boo" is delivered with an elongated "eee" ascending in pitch. The voice is positioned hard right in the stereo field. As this hook progresses, we hear an identical, delayed reverberant repeat gradually appearing hard left from silence, increasing in volume until level with the original. Here, Sioux's stripper persona is quite literally playing "Peek-A-Boo" with the audience: at first hidden, and then revealed stage left. We hear all this during the first two minutes of the song: the dramatic; "show time" introduction; the mechanical, radiophonic "zoetrope-like" backward rhythm sample; the "staged" voice; as well as the nod to polka, vaudeville, and Piaf; and the interpolation of Armstrong's Jeepers Creepers.

The embodiment of early cinema in "Peek-A-Boo" fittingly continued into the video, whereby Sioux is cast as a lone, yet glamorous film star figure, the invasive camera films her lip-synching in extreme close-up. Here, Sioux's Brooks-inspired screen persona is realized, as Margaret McCarthy noted of the way Brooks was often framed, "In many such shots her [Lulu's] head exceeds the filmic frame, as if Lulu's countenance could only be partially contained."[28] Shadow shots feature regularly throughout, particularly in scenes where we see the Banshees perform on "impossible" instruments, including a twisted, surrealist brass contraption, precisely the kind featured in Hollaender's "Dungeon Ballet"—and in masquerade masks. Finally, there are clear references to John Robertson's 1920 silent classic *Dr Jekyll and Mr Hyde* (1920) with the separation of Sioux as "star of stage and screen" from her Banshees, the four of them parading around in Weimar-style top hats and bow ties—and in shadow play throughout.

"Peek-A-Boo"—a damning critique on the sex industry via Sioux's first-person narrated, objectified stripper— is *Peepshow*'s exposition. The dramatic "show time" introduction, the construction of a panoramic peep show "stage," the creation of such an evocative protagonist, the centrality of scopophilia to the lyrical diegesis; the visual allusion to Weimar-era silent film classics: G. W. Pabst's *Diary of a Lost Girl* and *Pandora's Box* and the prostitution narratives central to both. In *Visual Pleasure and Narrative Cinema*, Laura Mulvey states,

> In their traditional, exhibitionist role, women are simultaneously looked at and displayed, with their

appearance coded for strong visual and erotic impact so that they can be said to connote *to-be-looked-at-ness*. Woman displayed as sexual object is the leitmotif of erotic spectacle . . . she holds the look, plays to and signifies male desire.[29]

"Peek-A-Boo" certainly conjures up this very cinematic aesthetic, but also ruptures the fantasy of male desire: yes, Sioux's stripper describes her "to-be-looked-at-ness" with lines such as "furtive eyes peep out of holes," but she also mocks her viewers, describing their "flaccid ego"—one of just two double-tracked vocal lines in the entire song—and describes them as "beguiled." In cinema, this flipping of the traditional gaze is a rare perspective. "Peek-A-Boo," for all its un-pigeonhole-able-ness, is not *Peepshow*'s "odd one out" but its lynchpin: a mature, accomplished consolidation of cinematic influence, political standpoint, socio-historical imagery, and musical form.

Noir

[SANDY]: Jeffrey? Why?
[JEFFREY]: I'm seeing something that was always hidden.
I'm involved in a mystery. I'm in the middle of a mystery.
And it's all a secret.
— *Blue Velvet*

[MIRANDA] He showed me one day what he called his
killing-bottle. I'm imprisoned in it. Fluttering against the
glass. Because I can see through it I still think I can escape.
I have hope. But it's all an illusion.
— *The Collector*

Such is the inextricable nature of film noir with wider cinema that it is one of the most debated areas in film theory. An early attempt at defining film noir was made in 1955 by French critics Borde and Chaumeton. They suggested, "It is the presence of crime which gives *film noir* its most constant characteristic. 'The dynamism of violent death' is how Nino Frank evoked it," and argued film noir as featuring "qualities such as nightmarish, weird, erotic, ambivalent, and cruel."[1] It is the latter component of Borde and Chaumeton's noir that Severin conceptualized in "The Killing Jar," inspired by his "unhealthy obsession with the mechanics of cruelty. A vastly underrated vice."[2] Sioux too was fascinated with the violence of death, as she said, "I suppose I've always been very interested in crime, especially when I was very young. Some girls were into dolls, but I was always reading really gruesome murder stories."[3]

Film theorists have considered noir as everything from "films with a gloomy atmosphere"[4] to the "hard-boiled detective film"[5]; yet, the presence of a crime, usually a murder, is noir's most recognizable trait. Borde and Chaumeton noted crime and death as intrinsic to noir and, of course, Sioux and Severin were fascinated with both. Stylistically, though, film noir features a more complex set of codes than the crime and the investigation; Doll and Faller suggested eight characteristics that make up "the iconography of the genre"[6] to include

> low-key lighting, claustrophobic framing, shadows and/or reflections, unbalanced compositions, and great depth of field . . . urban landscapes; costuming . . . and most often rain-soaked environments.[7]

Doll and Faller argued that such stylistic elements "take precedence over plot"[8] in terms of interpretation and meaning. In this chapter, I conceptualize "The Killing Jar" as a classic example of noir, since like noir, its stylistic coding is more prominent than its narrative. For example, six of Doll and Faller's codes are heavily embedded in the track:

a. low-key lighting deduced from the "midnight" setting;

b. claustrophobic framing via the lyrical and aural representation of the killing jar;

c. a shadow is present in the narrative, and also personified;

d. unbalanced composition of instruments, particularly in verse two;

e. depth of field is constructed with lengthy time-based signal processing;

f. urban landscape (the city of Amsterdam) as the initial locality.

Even with the absence of a detective and investigation in the narrative of "The Killing Jar," the focus on cruelty and death coupled with such heavy stylistic coding results in the track's classic noir presentation. In saying that, however, nothing about "The Killing Jar" points or alludes to Doll and Faller's recognition of costumes. Their final code, that of rain-soaked environments, can, however, be found in "The Killing Jar." The track certainly evokes a *wet* environment: most of the setting is next to a body of water, there is also a wishing well nearby and other indicators including lightening and rust suggest rain, not to mention the swathes of reverb across instruments resulting in a "wet" mix.

Film noir has long proliferated from its roots in moody, 1940s crime genre, and while "The Killing Jar" features explicit reference to these origins of noir, it also resembles later, postmodern takes on the genre. In a rare reflection on Siouxsie and the Banshees' two-decade-long career, Sioux described the band's overall aesthetic, "It's not buckets of blood, it's more the tension of blood splashed on a daisy in the sunshine."[9] This conflation of violence and nature is integral to "The Killing Jar," the second of Peepshow's singles[10] and, arguably, one of Severin's most accomplished and memorable songs. The poetic juxtaposition of violence—with words like scything, rage, roaring, punches, cuts, crushed—with nature (twisted roots, water, the "blue midnight flare," lightning, and fireflies) is quintessentially Siouxsie and the Banshees. Such a vivid aesthetic is also inherent to the work of postmodern noir auteur director David Lynch, particularly his contrasting of underworld street violence and moral decay with the unforgiving brutality of nature in Blue Velvet (1986). While Michael Atkinson recognized in Lynch's "most inspired tableau, a vision of 1950s LIFE magazine-style kitchen convenience and Dantean grue,"[11] Betsy Berry revealed that in Blue Velvet Lynch

> reveals two very separate worlds: the real world, that which we can see and hear and touch; and a subconscious, dream world which must remain hidden, so potentially dark and violent are its wanderings.[12]

That Siouxsie and the Banshees were, like Lynch, "obsessed by the neuroses of suburbia"[13] is well documented but, more than that, the band were disgusted by the mundane banalities of suburban life and the homogenized, conformist lifestyles promoted by it. This is a band originally united by their suburban escape, yet they frequently—albeit metaphorically—returned only to remind themselves of the horrors contained within it.

At the core of noir is the femme fatale, a natural cinematic progression from the Weimar "New Woman." Borde and Chaumeton noted the femme fatale as "Frustrated and deviant, half predator, half prey, detached yet ensnared, she falls victim to her own traps."[14] Of all noir's aesthetics, it is this aspect of entrapment that Severin quite literally encapsulated on "The Killing Jar," as he stated,

> A killing jar is a device used by butterfly collectors to contain and ultimately kill their specimen. . . . An emotional relationship snuffed out until it is merely a prized possession or keep sake.[15]

While parallels might be drawn between the femme fatale and the female vocal in "The Killing Jar," Sioux's role in the song is that of narrator, and while the narrative focuses on two male lead protagonists, it is never quite clear whose hand is around the killing jar. The lyrics retain an ambiguousness, which Severin applied to many songs from the beginning of the band's career, as he said, "There's an ambiguity in every song in some way or another."[16]

From another filmic angle, "The Killing Jar" bears more than passing resemblance to John Fowles's novel

The Collector (1963) (and, in turn, William Wyler's 1965 film adaptation). In this London and Sussex-based tale of obsession and torture, Ferdinand Clegg is a simple, lonely young man who rattles around in a large, Sussex country house (again, not unlike Berry House) spending much of his time as an amateur lepidopterist, collecting, examining, and displaying butterflies. The focus of the plot is on his kidnapping of art student Miranda Grey and much of the narration unfolds from a dank, stone cellar, the site of Grey's captivity. Unsurprising then is that Severin took inspiration from Fowles's novel, since it is from this horrific place of Grey's incarceration that Fowles deconstructs the intricate mechanics of cruelty over a prolonged and torturous psychological game of cat and mouse. Certainly, *The Collector* features foregrounded elements of horror and thriller, but ultimately, its noir aesthetics underpin the story, as Borde and Chaumeton suggested, "Sordidly or bizarrely, death always comes at the end of a tortured journey. In every sense of the word a *noir* film is a film of death."[17] "The Killing Jar" is, however, neither a homage to nor reiteration of Fowles's novel, but rather an allusion to Fowles's successful harnessing of the aesthetics of cruelty via the same butterfly preservation metaphor. As Severin suggested, "The use of the word killing jar in the song is used as a metaphor for controlled violence."[18] In "The Killing Jar," the insect suffocation device is depicted musically as well as lyrically via, quite paradoxically, one of the more melodic and accessible Siouxsie and the Banshees singles.

As "The Killing Jar" opens with a lazy reggae beat against a sparse and reverberant soundscape, within the first few seconds the studio constructivism of "Peek-A-Boo" feels a million miles away. Yet *Peepshow*'s first two tracks are tightly bound by the peep show itself: "Peek-A-Boo" takes place inside the claustrophobic peep show arena, whereas "The Killing Jar" begins as a commentary on the peep show's seedy, outdoor environmental situ, as Severin recalled of the lyrics,

> I'd had the first lines for ages. On a night out in Amsterdam I got into a taxi that was decorated with the most hideously lurid porno/escort cards and the driver was a really, greasy scuzzball who had been given a good whack with the "ugly" stick.[19]

This opening line is a great example of Severin's construction of storyworlds and the immediacy with which he establishes settings and the agendas of protagonists. The first word—"down"—lets us know this story takes place somewhere beneath the perceived surface of reality, in an underworld of sorts. The "ugly man" is an unlikable protagonist who is seeking sustenance; again, in an underworld environment, this must be something forbidden or illegal. Almost as soon as this Amsterdam red light district situ is established, however, it suddenly disappears, replaced by a nighttime setting in woodland—as depicted by "roots"—and near to a body of water. "The Killing Jar" features two male protagonists: the earlier ugly man and another, who bears a glass hand, quite likely inspired by the "Demon With A Glass Hand" episode of *The Outer Limits* (1964).[20] To whom the glass hand belongs is never revealed, but the critical role of this protagonist to the narrative structure is denoted by a recurring chime leitmotif animating the hand as it emerges from the water (0.28 and 0.32). This recurrent leitmotif is one aspect of a much broader musical allusion to classical romanticism, the perfect accompaniment to a 1940s noir-inspired narrative. Martin McCarrick's cello is foregrounded throughout, underscoring the track with a lush, romantic melodic progression that sweeps across Budgie's shuffling hi-hat while rendering Klein's guitar accents to the background.

The "golden age" of Hollywood film[21] relied heavily upon romanticism to convey its most emotive storylines; the conventional orchestration of strings playing harmonies in minor keys routinely dramatized depictions of loss, grief, love (in separation and in unity), sorrow, and elation. Kathryn Kalinak defined romanticism as a genre that

> privileges melody, an accessible musical structure for untrained listeners . . . privileging of the melody in the score meshed nicely with the privileging of narrative in the classical Hollywood style. Romanticism also had at its disposal the concept of the leitmotif, an extremely adaptable mechanism for accessing listeners, unifying the score and responding to a film's dramatic needs.[22]

Hollywood's leaning on the crutch of romanticism resulted in a set of film music norms and conventions that prevail in film to this day. As Claudia Gorbman noted, narrative film's "core musical lexicon has tended to remain conservatively rooted in romantic tonality, since its purpose is quick and efficient signification to a mass audience."[23] On the one hand, McCarrick's melancholic cello in "The Killing Jar" pays homage to romanticism, yet on the other, there is a strong sense of irony in the way this beautiful underscore is juxtaposed with a narrative depicting such vicious cruelty. Again, this epitomizes Siouxsie and the Banshees' core aesthetic; even at their most accessible, nothing is all it seems on the surface.

The patience with which Ferdinand Clegg tortures Miranda in *The Collector* and the intolerable anticipation this invokes in the audience is similarly constructed in "The Killing Jar" via a two-stage pre-chorus. At 0.42 the song breaks into an urgent double time; McCarrick's cello suddenly moves from its relaxed, dreamy melodic underscore into choppy staccato eighths as Budgie meanders around a complex tom roll. We appear to have stayed by the body of water during the pre-chorus, since the introduction of a reverberant Güiro to the right of the stereo field emulates the sound of croaking frogs.

At 0.55, we hear one of the most powerful segments on *Peepshow*: this has less to do with the lyrical allusion to Nitzsche and Bono's "Needles and Pins"[24] and more to do with the rhythmic coalescence of Budgie's sudden move from floor tom to whip-crack snare with Severin's taut hold on an upper octave eighth-note progression. During this intense pre-chorus section (0.55–1.09), the unbearable strain of slow suffocation is aurally constructed; if McCarrick's cello symbolizes the beauty of the captured, then Severin's suddenly foregrounded, heavily chorused bass squeezes the life from it simultaneous to Sioux's femme fatale observing a male protagonist "gasping for air."

Verse two features an equally evocative musicality. Following an upbeat instrumental break where Klein's "insect-like guitar"[25] mimics bugs inside the jar and Budgie's reverberant, clicking temple blocks alludes to water drops in the wishing well (1.24–1.36), we hear a key sonic diversion. Minus the guitar and cello, Severin's circular, chorusing bass is isolated (1.37) and, against the sparse vocals, is comparatively contained thus aurally representing the interior of the killing jar itself. Sioux's vocals, however, are treated entirely differently. Wispy and reverberant, a little chorus and plenty of reverb with lengthy decay has been applied resulting in extended sibilance, particularly noticeable on words like "soft" (1.38) and "shadow" (1.39).[26] This is one of many examples on *Peepshow* where the band weaves the technical aspects of filmmaking seamlessly into both the lyrical and musical progressions, for this focus on the shadow is a strong *chiaroscuro* reference, a renaissance painting technique later realized in Weimar film and integral to the visual aspects of noir.[27]

But there is something else going on. In the first two lines of verse two, this shadow is personified in both size and emotive expression in what Kathrin Fahlenbrach recognized in film sound design as "metaphorical mapping,"[28]

an effective mechanism, both in production and in reception of films, to synaesthetically fuse the appearance of figures, objects, and spaces with cognitive and emotional meanings on the level of narration.[29]

This complex sound design tool is exactly what Severin applies to verse two, not just to bring the shadow to life but also to throw another proverbial spanner into the narrative works of this multilayered noir. For this oxymoronic ascription of such emotive and violent actions to the "soft" shadow—the "metaphorical mapping" Fahlenbrach notes—vindicates his narrator, even at the point she narrates apparently holding the killing jar in her own hands. Of course, the death itself is reserved for the chorus (2.32), and what better way to underpin it than with a twist on the ubiquitous Christian burial service reading:

> In the sweat of thy face shalt thou eat bread,
> till thou return unto the ground;
> for out of it wast thou taken:
> for dust thou *art*,
> and unto dust shalt thou return.[30]

Similar to David Bowie's "Ashes to Ashes"[31] (to which this chorus also alludes) the word play in "The Killing Jar" is equivocal. The use of "rust" (2.33) in place of "dust" links back to the pre-chorus where a male protagonist is trapped inside the wishing well, for this is a place where coins are thrown and inevitably corrode with time. Again, the replacement of "ashes" with "gashes" (2.35) appears apt in terms of rhyming, although this presentation is ambiguous at best; do we have two deaths here? Because on the one hand, we have a death by suffocation, as depicted via the protagonist "gasping for air" (1.02, 2.23) the "snuffing out" (1.57) of his fury and the resulting "muffled sighs" (2.14), not to mention the killing jar itself. Yet on the other, the cutting of the hand, the scything of roots, and resultant gashes are inconsistent with suffocation; these indicate a bloodier demise commensurate with a stabbing.

Unlike much film noir, the presence of the detective or any form of investigation is absent from this tale of death. This lack of formal resolution—the track moves through a middle eight (2.59–3.26) repeating the main chorus hook followed by a lengthy coda (3.27–end)—only serves to complicate the already ambiguous circumstances: Who has died? And how? Because ultimately, "The Killing Jar" leaves us hanging in the kind of suspense exploited by all great noirs: *who dunnit?*

Musical

[DOROTHY]: You're the best friends anybody ever had. It's funny, but I feel as if I've known you all along, but I couldn't have, could I?
[SCARECROW]: I don't see how. You weren't around when I was stuffed and sewn together, were you?
— *The Wizard of Oz*

[MARLOW] There was something odd about that journey. Something not quite right. Something I still dream about. I saw the scarecrow.
— *The Singing Detective*

[NAN ADAMS] I saw him again, and then again, on the long, straight stretch through Virginia. Just standing there. Not menacing, really. If anything, drab, a little mousy. Just a shabby, silly-looking scarecrow man.
— *The Twilight Zone*

With its chorus allusion to Victor Fleming's *The Wizard of Oz* (1939) and conceptual influence drawn from Dennis Potter's teleplay *The Singing Detective* (1986), "Scarecrow" features aspects of the film musical genre extending beyond the reference implied by its central protagonist. Severin himself described *Peepshow* and the subsequent tour's overall aesthetic as "a bit like a musical"[1] and nowhere on *Peepshow* is this more apparent than in "Scarecrow." Certainly *Peepshow* exuded similar stylistic charisma to Bob Fosse's Weimar musical love note *Cabaret* (1972), but the record features a breadth and depth of musicality and poetic devices too complex to be considered only as historical homage.

The term "musical" was not broadly accepted until 1930–31[2] when a sudden explosion of song-and-dance films featuring lavish productions and theatrical choreography proliferated in Hollywood and beyond. For the next two decades, film musical reigned supreme; its blending of spectacle, love stories and colorful *mise en scène*, as well as direct-to-audience camera shots proved, as Pramaggiore and Wallis noted, "The perfect showcase for cinema's magic, thanks to its uncanny ability to integrate character-driven romances with visual and aural sensation."[3] The genre made stars out of actors like Fred Astaire and Ginger Rogers, and consolidated the Marx Brothers' vaudeville and Broadway careers with big screen musical classics including *Animal Crackers* (1932) and *A Night at the Opera* (1935). This "golden age" of film musical featured dozens of movies now canonized, including *Oklahoma* (1955) and *The King and I* (1956).

Musical film relied on established Hollywood convention perhaps more so than any other film genre. Despite the opulent backdrops and exuberant performances, the genre featured predictable narratives, simple characters, and relied heavily upon sentimentality. To that end, Fleming's *The Wizard of Oz* was an anomaly. But before discussing the relevance of his musical to Siouxsie and the Banshees' "Scarecrow" let's first consider the scarecrow as protagonist in a broader context.

In wider popular culture, scarecrows are often portrayed as hapless, comedic personalities; in 1980s children's television, Jon Pertwee's troublemaking scarecrow Worzel Gummidge epitomized this inept character. Such depictions are likely a result of an early portrayal by Buster Keaton in *The Scarecrow* (1920). Keaton plays a farm assistant in the film who, when chased by the farmer and his dog, dons the scarecrow's clothes and hangs on a post as a decoy. This "scarecrow as disguise" device also featured in F. W. Murnau's *Nosferatu* (1922); as Knock escapes from the psychiatric ward, he is pursued by a mob that has mistaken him for Nosferatu. A lone silhouette in a field is shot through *vignette*, which is revealed to be a scarecrow; this figure is promptly torn apart by one of the townsmen and as the rest of the mob catch up and throw the scarecrow's clothes into the air, the "effect is that of a 'dance of death.'"[4] Later depictions of the scarecrow featured more sophisticated aspects of disguise, concealment, and ambiguity. Dr. Jonathan Crane, aka The Scarecrow, first appeared in DC's Batman comics in the 1940s as a professor of psychiatry specializing in fears and phobias. His scarecrow was a terrifying, masked alter ego that used "fear gas" to incite hallucinations and nightmares in his victims. Walt Disney later capitalized on this "scarecrow-as-alter-ego" character in *The Scarecrow of Romney Marsh* (1963), a vigilante alter ego of Dr. Christopher Syn, the leader of a gang of smugglers who fight against the King's naval press gangs. This scarecrow character gallops around the Sussex countryside on various rescue missions all the while deceiving the government.

Possibly the most disturbing construction of a scarecrow-like figure manifests in Robin Hardy's British occult horror *The Wicker Man* (1973). Sioux likened the film's rural, yet rugged countryside setting and village charm to *Peepshow*'s pre-production location of Ardingly. While *The Wicker Man* has been classified as horror, it is a film, as Leon Hunt rightly suggested, that "seems designed to accommodate a range of positions and readings."[5] For all its unease and suspense, drama, and horror, *The Wicker Man* also works as a musical featuring songs and performances that subordinate the narrative.

Severin referred to Dennis Potter's *The Singing Detective* (1986) as "a masterpiece"[6] and it was the final episode—"Who Done It"—of this critically acclaimed teleplay that fired the spark for "Scarecrow." Set in the countryside location of Forest of Dean, Gloucestershire, Potter's serial is based on lead protagonist Marlow, who is hospitalized with severe psoriasis. *The Singing Detective* is often read as noir thriller, yet "the who dunnit rationale of the story is . . . subordinate."[7] Potter's teleplay nonetheless blends a 1940s film noir aesthetic with elements of melodrama and surrealism and as Kenneth Pellow noted, the serial is

> a stunning example of postmodern pastiche, replete with flashbacks, jump cuts, half-dissolves, voice-overs, and superimposition . . . . Prominent among such devices is the repeated intrusion of songs . . . being imagined by the main character.[8]

In "Who Done It," Marlow experiences flashbacks to his childhood. He takes a train journey alone through the countryside, and as the train passes through a field, Marlow sees a scarecrow who suddenly springs to life singing Al Johnson's 1930s jazz classic "After You've Gone." As the episode unfolds, the scarecrow visits Marlow in hospital leaving a trail of maggots behind him as he shuffles through the hospital reception; Marlow later has another flashback to his childhood train journey where he sees a silhouette of the scarecrow on a hill. In one of the most orchestrated musical scenes in the entire series, Marlow drifts off again and is suddenly transported to a jazz club. The Henry Hall Orchestra perform a cabaret version of children's song "The Teddy Bears Picnic" as the montage of Marlow's past thoughts and dreams becomes enmeshed in the surrealist narrative. Here, the lasting influence of this specific episode on *Peepshow* is clear, for a lyrical allusion to "The Teddy Bears Picnic" also features in the liner notes: "If you go down to the woods today you'll find that we're not there."[9] Potter's character is one of the most disturbing portrayals of a scarecrow on screen and it is this depiction that inspired *Peepshow*'s "Scarecrow" the most as ultimately, Potter's scarecrow character is a metaphor for childhood memories and the power of imagination and imaginary friends.

Siouxsie and the Banshees' "Scarecrow" does, however, conflate Potter's representation with musical film's most recognized incarnation. Academic studies of *The Wizard of Oz* agree that the scarecrow is a metaphor for the Western farmer, uneducated yet shrewd and with advanced common sense. The scarecrow is a complex, yet pivotal, character in Fleming's benchmark film musical and is also considered central to the widely accepted interpretation of *The Wizard of Oz* as a "sophisticated commentary on the political and economic debates of the Populist Era,"[10] specifically the US free silver movement of the late nineteenth century and its opposition to a deflationary gold standard. For political theorist Hugh Rockoff, the scarecrow

> brings to life a major theme of the free silver movement: that the people, the farmer in particular, were capable of understanding the complex theories that underlay the choice of a standard. They did not have to accept a monometallic gold standard simply because the experts said that it was necessary.[11]

While the scarecrow does not directly narrate or depict anything to do with gold or silver in the musical (aside from, along with the other characters, following the yellow brick road) this political interpretation is explicitly referenced in Siouxsie and the Banshees' "Scarecrow" chorus, where Sioux's protagonist refers to "gold and silver stitches." That Severin positions this in line three—straight after a clear reference to Dorothy's iconic wish "there's no place like home" in line two—suggests that the chorus alludes more strongly to the scarecrow in *The Wizard of Oz* than Potter's scarecrow in *The*

Singing Detective. These lyrics are a sophisticated merging of the scarecrow and later political interpretation, but there is something else in this extraordinary chorus that binds the entire narrative together literally and metaphorically. Just like in T. S. Eliot's poem, "The Hollow Men," the scarecrow has, alas, a "headpiece filled with straw."[12] The straw construction of the scarecrow requires him to be sewn together, which is portrayed in various ways throughout *The Wizard of Oz* in an obvious allusion to Eliot's poem, for all of Dorothy's friends are "hollow men" in one way or another.[13] However, in Siouxsie and the Banshees' "Scarecrow," Severin did not write about *sewing* gold and silver stitches, but *spinning* them. To make the allusions even more complex and layered, this is of course a reference to one of the most famous fairytales in history, that of *Rumpelstiltskin*,[14] and its central thematic, the miller's daughter turning straw into gold on a spinning wheel.

In *The American Film Musical*, Rick Altman argued that musical films feature a "fundamental dualistic structure."[15] He defined a four-stage structural framework in which film musicals work and "Scarecrow" also works when viewed through Altman's theoretical lens:

a. Altman argued that musical film "progresses through a series of paired segments matching the male and female leads."[16] Here, scenes are often cut between individual protagonists in order to show their simultaneous positions while they are separated on screen—the "Willow's Song" segment of *The Wicker Man* is a good example of this technique. While these paired segments are often portrayed through predictable, heteronormative connections—think

Captain Georg von Trapp and Maria in *The Sound of Music* (1965) or Mary Poppins and Bert in *Mary Poppins* (1964)—the more complex musical films feature ambiguous relationships. Altman theorized that a problem exists whereby traditional love stories do not form the central plot

> because they are too young or too wacky. In this situation one of two methods is commonly used to set the musical back on its couple-conscious course: 1) the young girl is paired with an older man (or men) who becomes her coconspirator(s) rather than an amorous partner (e.g. Judy Garland in The Wizard of Oz); or 2) a secondary pair are in love, the principles serving as catalysts.[17]

Throughout "Scarecrow," we hear the paired segments Altman describes play out. For example, in the first verse the narration flips to and fro from the position of the scarecrow trembling in the wind to Sioux's narrator—a young girl persona present with "others," who are depicted sleeping. In this song, the scarecrow is not the love interest of Sioux's young girl protagonist, but her coconspirator as Altman would suggest; this duality plays out explicitly in verse two where in the first line the young girl confides her secrets to the scarecrow. By line four, the conspiratorial relationship is further reinforced as the two are depicted alone and confiding in each other. This duality develops not just in the relationship but also in the simultaneous separation of the protagonists' settings, which is very simply, yet perfectly denoted in the first two verses. In verse one, the narration is from an indoor space; the narrating young girl protagonist is *here* with others, who are sleeping. By verse two, the narrator is outside on a hill and she reminds us that the "others" are *there* and still sleeping.

b. Altman argued that in terms of setting or *mise en scène*, shot selection, music, dance, and style, "each separate part of the [musical] film recapitulates the film's overall duality."[18] Musically and narratively, this duality evolves in "Scarecrow" perhaps more so than in any other track on *Peepshow*, reflecting Severin's deep understanding of filmic mechanisms across multiple genres, not least film musical. Let's think about the dualities present in the music. The track begins with a repetitive sample-trigger of chirpy crickets; that this sound is continuous is an illusion, since the gaps are masked with a delicate cymbal and a further, repeat decaying light percussive click. This combination of soft, reverberant sounds lends the track an outdoors summery atmosphere with the crickets alluding to countryside fields, yet the lyrics suggest the scarecrow is trembling "in the bitter wind" evoking a contradictory image of a cold winter (0.21). Here, an ambient descending synth glissando represents the wind as it wafts between the instruments; this effective atmospheric gesture continues throughout each verse.

The initial, peaceful outdoor soundscape, however, has already been interrupted by Jon Klein's guitar (0.07); its comparatively present, heavily delayed harmonics suddenly fill the foreground and create the perfect stage for Sioux's up-front vocal. Here, we hear a recapitulation of duality whereby the foregrounded instruments of guitar and vocal contrast the sparse, background soundscape: the delicate percussion and wind metaphor is set in opposition to Severin's bass (0.14), which is heavily chorused and delayed with lots of attack (though, in saying that, its hollow, decaying repeats reinforce a sense of quiet foreboding generated by the overall orchestration). Severin's dynamic bass swell motif at 0.50 perfectly alludes to the surreptitiousness of Sioux's escape as she slips out to meet her confidant, yet this bass line repeatedly swells only to fall away. The introduction of acoustic guitar and Budgie's snare brushes (0.59) anticipate the chorus, which marks the song's major contrasting duality. With an upbeat, galloping chorus (1.17) featuring further synth and guitar lines, this section presents a significant temporal, textural, and dynamic contrast to the sparse verses. Such a shift in gears again recapitulates the song's dualities, since the move into a double time gallop results in a (albeit illusionary) sense of an increase in speed, evoking *The Scarecrow of Romney Marsh* and Dr. Syn's smugglers galloping around the countryside on horseback.

Budgie's drum roll at 1.50 grinds the song almost to a halt, making way for a sparse, dualistic vocal and bass "call and answer," which acts as a break. In verse two, we hear a common film music technique in the use of Wagnerian *leitmotif*, "the assignment and repetition of short melodic phrases to signify key characters, places or social groups."[19] A delicate melody sounds (2.08) as a glockenspiel to denote the presence of Jack Frost, a personification of freezing winter cold. This foregrounding of a spine-tingling effect—a Herrmannian trope—sharply cuts through the distant, atmospheric background creating timbral contrast.

c. Altman suggests that "the basic sexual duality overlays a secondary dichotomy."[20] In this case, the atypical (non-sexual) relationship between lead protagonists in "Scarecrow" is the primary duality here, with the secondary dichotomy the connection between Sioux's narrator protagonist and her friends. On the one hand, our narrator has an initial strong sense of belonging with her group; she refers to "us" and "we" in the first verse and choruses. On the other hand, by the third verse our narrator is diverted away from the scarecrow. Her sense of belonging turns to resentment and her friends' disbelief in the scarecrow's existence leads to a conveyed sense of betrayal. It is here that "Scarecrow" begins to pull away from conventional musical, as elements of surrealism seep into the story.

d. In Altman's fourth aspect of musical's structural framework, he suggests of film musical's conclusions, "The marriage which resolves the primary (sexual) dichotomy also mediates between the two terms of the secondary (thematic) opposition."[21] Since "Scarecrow" features an atypical protagonist relationship structure, this resolution is not one of unity. Instead, "Scarecrow" diverts from the "happy ever after" resolution so integral to Hollywood musicals. Severin constructs—in a figment of the lead protagonist's imagination—a scene where a vengeful Sioux chastises her friends for disbelieving her tales of the scarecrow (3.06). She first imagines baking their bones before peeling a pastry top from a pie, then pouring gravy in their eyes. While all this takes place using traditional, albeit imaginary, structured narrative form, this sudden surrealist departure from the main verse/chorus is nonetheless so unforgettably graphic that the fantastical image—like so many from the Buñuel/Dalí partnership—is forged into our minds. Rudolf Kuenzli noted,

> The cinematic apparatus is used by surrealist filmmakers as a powerful means to realistically portray the symbolic order, which they then disrupt with shocking, terrifying images.[22]

And this is exactly the mechanism Severin uses to disrupt the narrative order of "Scarecrow." Any chance his "modern day fairytale"[23] had of ending "happily ever after" is brutally ruptured with this sudden, violent resolution: a hallmark not of film musical, but of surrealist paracinema. Inspired by David Bowie's "The Bewlay Brothers,"[24] Severin took pride in creating this verse, as he said "I loved getting that word [gravy] into a Banshees song in such a nasty context!"[25] In a further twist, Severin chose not to end "Scarecrow" at this moment, instead positioning this sharp narrative turn in verse three before steering it back on track. At almost a minute long, the coda of "Scarecrow" is lengthy, yet the galloping momentum is maintained by Klein's melodic guitar, one of the only phrases on *Peepshow* where the guitar features a traditional rock sound. Sioux's shrill vocal punctuates the heavily textured outro until 4.37 when the track finally subsides. The final, ambient outro of "Scarecrow" suggests that, just like Potter's scarecrow in *The Singing Detective*, our lead protagonist is only a figment of Sioux's imagination. Jack Frost's leitmotif returns (4.37), along with Klein's harmonics (4.42) heard at the beginning of track. At this point, we hear Sioux's soft, reverberant voice drifting through the mix (4.41–4.45).

Like Marlow's memories and Dorothy Gale's Emerald City adventure, there is the suggestion that "Scarecrow" was just a figure in her dream.

In film musical, songs are used as narrative interjections in order to consolidate meaning, whether in terms of relationships or protagonist predicament; Dorothy, for example, breaks into "Follow the Yellow Brick Road" as she is standing on its spiral starting point. Hollywood musical's narrative conservatism is such that songs are often positioned as naturally flowing from spoken exchanges. The difference with a musical like *The Singing Detective* is that its song interpolations are less devices for narrative scaffolding and more sharp, surrealist twists designed to suddenly throw the audience off the beaten track and into other unexpected, often disturbing dimensions. This complex layering of typically conservative musical structures and surrealism in order to denote temporal disruption is what Severin accomplishes in "Scarecrow." The track's rural soundscape evokes not only the site of the field scarecrow, but also the country village atmosphere of Ardingly; its woodland surrounds the perfect spot for a Teddy Bear's Picnic, albeit one missing Siouxsie and the Banshees.

Vaudeville

[WHIPSNADE]: You kids are disgusting! Staggering around here all day, reeking of popcorn and lollipops.
— *You Can't Cheat an Honest Man*

[AMY]: Listen, how would you like to go to the movies instead of the carnival?
[BUZZ]: The movies? What for?
[AMY]: It's the same carnival that went through Fairfield County, where they had all that trouble.
[BUZZ]: Terrific. Maybe we'll get a little action. Come on. You're not afraid to go, are you?
— *The Fun House*

Film owes much to the proto-cinematic theatrical art of vaudeville due to its ubiquity in the United States and Canada between 1880 and 1930. This cheap variety entertainment, which drew heavily from the circus, was popularized in the late nineteenth century; vaudeville acts including magicians, actors, jugglers, and musicians would perform as part of a single bill of entertainment in theaters, at fairgrounds, and carnivals across the United States.[1] Colorful and rowdy, the sensational, yet accessible experience afforded by vaudeville entertainment resulted in a proliferation of theaters and enterprises across the United States by the turn of the twentieth century. Vaudeville performances were often staged in amusement parks "characterized by . . . dynamism—its brash colors, constant noise, and the continual movement of people and machinery,"[2] where the diverse form of variety entertainment found a natural synergy. One such place was Coney Island, New York—the heart of America's burgeoning fairground and vaudeville entertainment industry. Taking in Luna Park, the amusement destination was "an environmental phantasmagoria combining characteristics of the . . . county fair, vaudeville and circus."[3] Its expansive size and breadth of amusements drew vacation crowds from across the United States, but its feature attraction was the world's first carousel, built by Charles Looff and installed in 1875. Such was the draw of Coney Island that in the late nineteenth century, dozens of short films were made at the location including the American Mutoscope and Biograph Company's *Ariel Slide at Coney Island* (1897) and *Riding on the Merry-Go-Round* (1897). Edison's *Merry-Go-Round* (1898) was also filmed at a picnic park in New York,[4] cementing the carousel as a prominent cinematic motif. As Fried noted in *A Pictorial History of the Carousel* there is no difference between carousels and merry-go-rounds, other than the origin of the terms.[5]

In the early twentieth century, the lines between vaudeville and cinema blurred. Proto-cinematic "photoplays" would often act as "chasers," segues between live vaudeville acts,[6] before motion pictures broke away from the vaudeville theater in the form of Harry Davis's Nickelodeon.[7] Unsurprisingly, cinema took some of vaudeville's biggest stars with it, including W. C. Fields[8]—a San Francisco Orpheum "tramp juggler" who made his name juggling "hats, cigar boxes—anything he could get his hands on."[9] Charlie Chaplin was another—albeit less successful—vaudevillian who, along with Stan Laurel, cut his teeth touring the United States with the Karno vaudeville company prior to entering silent film. Fields and Chaplin were two vaudevillians who successfully brought the spirit of vaudeville into film, particularly in the carnival-themed *You Can't Cheat an Honest Man* (1939) and *The Circus* (1928) respectively; the aesthetics of vaudeville—particularly in the form of its fairground and amusement park localities—are routinely depicted in film to this day. The inextricable marriage of the amusement park and film is, of course, the very concept of twentieth-century cinema's most successful company: Disney.[10] *Peepshow*'s "Carousel" manages to blend the amusement park and film in two key ways. Indeed, the track simultaneously

a. Reflects the evolution of the fairground and carousel on screen, and

b. Embodies a proto-cinematic aesthetics of attractions as opposed to a defined narrative.

First, let's think about point "a": how the track reflects the carousel on screen via some of Siouxsie and the Banshees' known film influences.

A key reference to the carousel in film is found in Disney's adaptation of the Ray Bradbury novel *Something Wicked This Way Comes* (1983); undoubtedly an influence on *Peepshow* since it is also the title of one of the B-sides of "The Killing Jar" single.[11] The plot centers on Will and Jim, two young schoolboys who encounter a travelling fairground: Mr. Dark's Pandemonium Carnival. At one point, the boys encounter a carousel marked "out of order" and later, they witness the carnival manager Mr. Cooger aboard the carousel. Through its colorful, whirling spins Will and Jim watch until Mr. Dark stops the carousel and lifts Mr. Cooger from it who has turned into a little boy.

The lyrics in "Carousel" explicitly reference Tobe Hooper's *The Fun House* (1981)[12] and there are obvious links to be drawn. Early on in the film, four friends Amy, Buzz, Liz, and Richie head to a fairground, the entrance of which is adorned with a large red dragon painted on the veranda. Hooper juxtaposes common signifiers of fairground fun with aspects of revulsion: a sideshow with deformed "freak" animals and a "mutation" fetus in a display cabinet. Hooper plays heavily on the impending peril of our four intrepid friends, particularly when they are eventually trapped in the dark ghost train "Fun House" ride.

An attempt at disrupting the predictable narrative flow of such a ubiquitous Hollywood trope is found in David Lynch's *Eraserhead* (1977). For this bleak, surrealist-inspired tale of parenthood and fear, Lynch, along with composers Fats Waller and Peter Ivers, created a minimalist proto-industrial score. They juxtaposed stark, unrelenting environmental noise with silence to underscore the deep social anxiety of *Eraserhead*'s lead protagonist Henry Spencer. At one point, Henry's wife appears on a stage, disfigured with visible tumors on her face as sperm fall from the theater's rafters. Fairground calliope music circles around this portrayal of fear of the erosion of self through parenthood.

This association of the carousel with childhood also plays out in one of the most celebrated episodes of Rod Serling's *The Twilight Zone* (1959). "Walking Distance" follows Martin, a media executive, as he encounters himself as a young boy. The plot thickens as the adult Martin runs to the park where he finds himself as a twelve-year-old aboard a carousel. This episode was scored by Bernard Herrmann, who masterfully winds up the sound of fairground music into the classical underscore signifying regression from adult to child. It is precisely this Herrmannian, experimental interpolation of environmental sounds that we hear in "Carousel," as Severin stated: "Carousel is trying to remember what it's like when you're a child."[13] As "Walking Distance" closes, Rod Serling narrates,

> Like all men perhaps there'll be an occasion . . . when he'll look up from what he's doing and listen to the distant music of a calliope . . . and perhaps across his mind there'll flit a little errant wish that a man might not have to become old, never outgrow the parks and the merry-go-rounds of his youth.[14]

This reminiscing of youth was also expressed by Sioux, who stated in relation to "Carousel": "I have a lot of regret about that transition from being a child into adulthood, when a child stops looking at adults as 'big people.'"[15] The carousel and concomitant calliope music of the fairground was a mainstay Hitchcockian trope; the most memorable scene is that of the merry-go-round in *Strangers on a Train* (1951), cited by the Banshees as an inspiration for "Carousel."[16] In the film's iconic fairground scene, calliope music underscores dual diegeses. As Bruno follows Miriam onto the carousel for a few rotations, we hear a pipe organ playing the waltz "And the Band Played On." In a brief interpolation of musical theater, the song morphs from the carousel's calliope into a full scale sing-along as the characters spin round in one of the film's most foreboding scenes.

"Carousel," like opening track "Peek-A-Boo," is also a great example of *Caligarisme*, for its depiction of this mainstay fairground attraction is of both excitement and trepidation. Indeed, Weine's *Das Cabinet des Dr. Caligari* (1920) was the very first film to posit the fairground in this way with the Holstenwall Fair, that was visited by Dr. Caligari and his somnambulist Ceasare. Caligari's vaudevillian routine with his sleepwalking sidekick is hilarious entertainment, but there is an underlying sense of fear at the fair; this is the site of multiple recent murders and the implication of Caligari and/or Ceasare as perpetrators hangs over the film in a metaphorical shadow to match those visually constructed on set. Caligari also features the regression metaphor, as Adkinson states,

For adults [the fair] is a regression into childhood days, in which games and serious affairs are identical, real and imagined things mingle, and anarchical desires aimlessly test infinite possibilities.[17]

So, from the moment we jump aboard Siouxsie and the Banshees' "Carousel," we are slowly transported back in time from the pre-production location of Ardingly (as signified by the found sounds of "Carousel" captured by Sioux at the gypsy fairground in 1987). "Carousel" then takes us back a couple of years, stopping off at Mr. Dark's Pandemonium Carnival, then further back to Hooper's blacked-out Fun House ride. We travel further still through *The Twilight Zone* and Hitchcock's Hollywood classics, we hang around with Ceasare for a while at the Holstenwall Fair before suddenly truncating at turn-of-the-century vaudeville. That this vaudevillian journey takes place in reverse—we know this, since by the coda of "Carousel" the fairground experience is revealed to be a memory—is reference to both the backward and/or twisted motion of the carousel itself as depicted in many of the aforementioned films and the historical origin of the band's artistic inspiration. Narratively, the Banshees were masters at scaffolding creative sparks fired by what they saw at the movies last week with their deep knowledge of European history, literature, and cinema. "Carousel," therefore, epitomizes this sophisticated modus operandi at its conceptual and musical peak.

While we could pin "Carousel" anywhere along this trajectory line of the fairground in the cinematic arts, I argue that it belongs closer to the beginning (in vaudeville) that at the end (at the Pandemonium Carnival). Why? Because of its foregrounded lead instrument: the calliope.

Let's now think about point "b": how "Carousel" defies conventional narrative structures with its aesthetics of attractions. As with all *Peepshow*'s album tracks, when listening to "Carousel" we are transported to a specific environment. This time, the captivating storyworld of a turn-of-the-century fairground is created using an evocative narrative underpinned with extensive synthesis, found sounds and augmented with multiple—largely percussive—effects. In 1985, film theorists Tom Gunning and André Gaudreault coined the term cinema of attractions[18] in reference to "curiosity-arousing devices" of the fairground. They argued that where Hollywood cinema privileges narrative, which in turn creates a "barrier" to a full understanding of the cinema, early cinema and the proto-cinematic arts foregrounded novelty, exhibitionism, and "the act of display."[19] Gunning's cinema of attractions was intended to build on Russian film director and theorist Sergei Eisenstein's use of the word "attraction" to mean "sensual or psychological impact"[20] on the spectator when theorizing the theatrical arts. Eisenstein felt that theater should feature a "montage of attractions,"[21] a succession of spectacular and sensational impacts as opposed to a formal narrative structure.[22]

Turn-of-the-century peepshows, circus acts, vaudeville performances, dioramas, and camera tricks were inherently colorful, sensational, and peculiar, not to mention unpredictable, since many contrasting acts would often appear as part of the same bill.[23] Gunning and Gaudreault proposed a thematic typology of such acts of display. This, they called a "topoi of aesthetics of a cinema of attractions,"[24] which pinpointed a number of key shared attributes of the proto-cinematic arts to include:

a. visual experiences such as color, scopophilia, and the phenomenon of motion;

b. novelty, including oddities and freaks and sensational current events;

c. socially taboo subject matter dealing with the body, whether that be nudity, deformity, or death;

d. violent and/or aggressive sensations including speed, peril, impending threat, or danger.[25]

Let's take a moment to cross-reference Gunning and Gaudrealt's topoi with the lyrics in "Carousel." Of course, the track has got the lot: what we have here is not so much the narration of a story or sequence of events as depicted through narrative cinema, but a series of experiential aspects of a cinema of attractions. Both explicitly in its narrative and subliminally in its music, Siouxsie and the Banshees' "Carousel" transports us back to a proto-cinematic fairground in all its garish dynamism. As Sioux mentioned when suggesting that *Peepshow* conveyed a vaudevillian aesthetic, it is "a slightly garish vaudeville, of course."[26]

Fittingly, "Carousel" features the most complex orchestration on *Peepshow* and bears more resemblance to a John Cage composition than popular music of the era. Most of the music was written by Budgie, who said the track had "been around for ages"[27] before reaching completion during the *Peepshow* sessions. "Carousel" makes the most of percussion to create its fairground environment; long before film music, this use of percussive effects as descriptive music to reinforce narrative was routinely employed in vaudeville, as Rick Altman noted,

> Among vaudeville musicians, the drummer deserves special attention. Vaudeville . . . sound effects were produced by the musicians themselves. The vaudeville drummer is thus closer to the percussionist of a band playing descriptive music.[28]

The minimalist introduction synth line in "Carousel" features a woody marimba-like timbre; its wide stereo panning[29] and elongated envelope hypnotically lures us into the fairground. Slowly, fairground music is wound in to the mix, steadily approaching until level, then moved around the stereo field as if we are surveying the entrance to this amusement park, just as Amy, Buzz, Liz, and Richie did in *The Fun House*. Composer John Cage once said, "I have come, through my music, to enjoy the sounds that are in my environment wherever I am."[30] The fairground music of "Carousel" reflects this Cageian interpolation of found sounds—a technique also used by Bernard Herrmann—since the music was recorded by Sioux on her Dictaphone at a local gypsy fairground "that turned up in a nearby field. That's the sound of real Victorian engines all mangled up"[31] thus anchoring the track firmly in its pre-production locality of Ardingly.

The sound of the calliope—or steam pipe organ as it was known in the late nineteenth century—is integral to the fairground: its whistling waltzes designed to be heard high above noisy crowds and the clunky mechanics of the carousel, which are reconstructed here with stunning effect. The synthesized calliope of "Carousel" has been constructed from at least three sounds including a foregrounded pipe playing a four-note ascending arpeggio, a percussive glockenspiel or bell-like upper harmonic layer on the last three notes of each bar plus a reversed synth swell over the last two beats, which lends the calliope its sense of circular, nausea-inducing, and abnormally rotating motion. While the melody is in common time, its rhythm alludes to the classic 3/4 triplet motif in Herrmann's "Prelude and Rooftop" (1958)[32] and his alternating ascending and descending note progressions, which evoke confusion, mystery, and suspense.[33] An underpinning synth bass playing single root notes with a lengthy attack time off to the center left beautifully contrasts the calliope; it fades in simultaneous to the marimba-like opening synth fading out leaving the calliope foregrounded in the mix at the point of the first verse. It is during this complex opening soundscape that the Banshees extensive synthesis and sampling compositional technique becomes apparent, yet aside from the found sounds, every instrument is performed, as Severin pointed out,

> It's a bit funny to us, because we've always used really bizarre things. People don't even know what is guitar and bass on the records sometimes; they think it's a lot of synthesizers and weird effects and things. It is, but it's all played.[34]

This further substantiates my earlier argument about "Carousel" exemplifying the height of Siouxsie and the Banshees' creativity, since in 1987, it would have been so much easier to simply sample such effects and incorporate them into the track, rather than creating them from scratch on instruments. This performance of "weird effects" is used in "Carousel" to augment the sensational, experiential aspects of the fairground and there are a number of points in the track where the method is particularly effective. Let's listen to the first verse (0.41–1.37). One carefully positioned effect is that of the synthesized vibraslap[35] (0.57), which enters hard right. Shortly after, a delayed (occurring momentarily later) copy of the effect appears centered in the mix and highlights impending peril. That the decay time of this vibraslap strike is elongated simultaneously to a sharp descent in pitch perfectly emulates the narrative: this is the sound of the dragon rollercoaster diving and soaring on its tracks although the sound returns later in the track, albeit heavily processed and disconnected from the narrative. Another example is found at 1.23. Here, "their tiny hands" line is double tracked, reinforcing the presence of a group of fairground helpers. A forebodingly slow, creaking helicopter-like motor sound is wound in at 1.26 hard right with a delayed copy hard left: it is too late—the rollercoaster is moving along its tracks and there is no turning back. That this movement occurs after the experience of the dragon soaring and diving in the lyrics only reinforces the surrealist notion that we are experiencing this fairground in some sort of dream, memory, or hallucination where all temporalities are distorted.

At 2.06, a swirling, ghost-like noisy guitar reverb is brought up in the mix to the right then moves to the center, only to then decay. These circling, swooshing sounds—the sort of sounds heard in a ghost train—are almost certainly created with Klein's guitar through his Morley AutoFlange.[36] The sense of approaching, impending danger is created with Budgie's cymbals, which enter at 2.02 hard right. Although placed low in the mix, the cymbals subtly inject a sense of foreboding into the track like an increasing heartbeat.

As "Carousel" progresses, its orchestration intensifies. The mechanics of the carousel—usually quieted by its accompanying calliope—are emulated at 2.22. Here, a sharp, metallic, mechanical sound effect likely generated from an analogue synthesizer[37] is positioned center left as we approach the carousel's "snarling horse." This same sound reappears at 2.25 centered, and yet again at 2.33, this time as an extended and prolonged effect. Both narratively and sonically, we approach and board the carousel as its "motor whirrs" before we hear the return of the rollercoaster motor motif from earlier in the track. Just before the ride begins, we are again reminded that all is not what it seems and this is possibly a dream (nightmare?) or hallucination. A stunning construction of experiential madness "inside your head" is heard at 2.55 where Sioux's vocal is aggressively panned left and right simultaneous to a descending glissando on "whirl": this signifies (a) the fairground is imagined, and (b) we are descending into madness.

Quite appropriately, the ride on the carousel is aggressive. Both the speed of the ride and the temporality of its duration are disrupted by Sioux's lyrics referring to both its roundabout rotation and the memory of the rider. Initially, Budgie's rhythm alludes to a 3/4 waltz with a three-note pattern (3.10) that breaks into a steady 4/4 after a few bars. The nauseous spinning of the carousel is depicted once more by Klein's guitar; the heavily flanged effect swooshes around for the duration of the coda before fading out as the introductory minimalist synth line returns (3.58). We are starting to come round from this nightmare. As the fairground music is wound back in, we hear a percussive creaking low in the mix that progressively slows, signifying the carousel grinding to a halt before the entire track suddenly truncates.

This precise sonic augmenting of the fairground experience is only one aspect of the functionality of "Carousel." What makes "Carousel" so convincing is the consolidation of this evocative soundscape with the positioning of the listener as central to its narrative storyworld. Sioux and her Banshees have long deserted this dreamy fairground leaving *you*, the listener, as lead protagonist in what they predicted would turn into a nightmare. And—as Sioux tells you with not a shred of sympathy—there is no escape. Sioux's lead vocal in "Carousel" is louder in the mix than on any other track on the album: it is as if she is narrating this story from another place entirely, such is the vocal's detachment from the rest of the fairground action. Couple this with the heavy compression and immaculate diction; Sioux narrates this story directly to you, softly whispering this nightmarish scenario of impending danger into your ear. That she does so in such a slow, careful, and unforgiving manner only exacerbates the sense of isolation: what is depicted so perfectly in this track is environmental realism. Here *you* are, in the middle of a colorful, swirling, curling fairground in all its "lurid hue," about to experience the most hellish ride where all your nightmares come true. Like the best film directors, Sioux manages to create a horrific scenario by planting thoughts in the listener's mind without explicitly depicting anything violent. This aesthetics of disconcertion forms the underpinning to the fairground as simultaneously joyful and horrifying, a place of wonder and fright, and—as she so beautifully surmises in the track's extended coda—of nostalgia and nightmare.

"Carousel" is a classic example of how the Banshees manage to time travel, how they take us listeners on historical, sonic journeys. "Carousel" is perfectly positioned at the nexus of vaudeville and cinema: its direct filmic influences are obvious, but the calliope, found sounds, and duality of a cinema of attractions and cinema's later post-war Hollywood realization of the fairground, lends "Carousel" its paracinematic feel. Sioux may explicitly reference Tobe Hooper's trashy *The Fun House*, and the heavily textured circulation of the track's carousel certainly consolidates a diegesis of distorted memories, as famously depicted in both *The 5000 Fingers of Dr. T* and *Strangers on a Train*. Stylistically, however, "Carousel" is not the story of—in typical Hollywood style—wholesome, good-time middle class kids in peril. The track's Cageian found sounds, its anchoring in Ardingly fairground, its blunt, evocative depictions of vivid colors and the contorted bodies of dwarfism perfectly illustrate a series of attractions inherent to the turn-of-the-century fairground.

Western

[HARMONICA]: When you hear a strange sound,
drop to the ground.
— *Once Upon a Time in the West*

[THE GOOD]: Every gun makes its own tune.
— *The Good, the Bad and the Ugly*

In 1989, Siouxsie and the Banshees discussed the origins of "Burn-Up" as inspired by "a show off the TV, a programme about New Orleans"[1] that featured a brass-oriented "funeral march."[2] Sioux recorded what she described as a "drone"[3] directly from the TV and, as Budgie stated,

> from that, it became a train—a train that was about to collide. Then the lyrics are starting to make some sense, as well. Martin (McCarrick) was playing his cello like a fiddle and banging his foot as it gets faster and faster.[4]

Directly acknowledging "Burn-Up" as a song that took "a very cinematic push in a certain direction,"[5] Sioux also described this musical construction of a "train out of control. The tracks run out and it tries to stop itself."[6] Conceptually, this train is one of a number of heavily Western-coded motifs heard in "Burn-Up," but the musical structuring of the train collision grounds the track in the very earliest forms of cinematic spectacle. Indeed, the locomotive was "the number one star of silent film."[7]

As twentieth-century film evolved, so too did the action-packed blockbuster, heavily reliant upon violence and spectacular crashes, explosions, and other catastrophic events. This now ubiquitous genre owes much to American inventor George Hale and his 1904 attraction *Hale's Tours and Scenes of the World*.[8] This amusement park attraction formed the carriage of a railway car in which patrons could see, hear, and feel the simulated movement of the carriage as it traversed various scenes depicted by moving picture. It was one of the first sites for the experience of motion picture, as the first Nickelodeon in America did not exist until 1905.[9] A mechanical belt beneath the carriage seats emulated the sound and feel of the railroad tracks giving the patrons the feeling of perpetual motion. At the turn of the twentieth century, such a train ride was unattainable to most Americans, as Raymond Fielding suggested,

> In this first decade of the twentieth century, the railroad train was the only mechanical means for transporting passengers and freight over land that had been extensively developed . . . for most of the economic lower class, a ride on a railroad train and Pullman car was prohibitively expensive and was, therefore, exotic in appeal.[10]

Hale's Tour, therefore, brought a sensational experience to the masses, not least since it was franchised in 1906. George Hale, therefore, was largely responsible for introducing motion pictures to Asia, South America, and Europe.[11] *Hale's Tours and Scenes of the World* can also be cited as the first railroad-oriented motion pictures to simulate speed, but this focus on the railway in motion picture began even earlier. The Lumiére Brothers' *Arrival of a Train at La Ciotat* (1895), for example, was one of the first—and most iconic—in a long line of railroad-focused films. At the time, this short fifty-second clip instilled terror and panic in audiences, who were convinced that the featured locomotive was heading straight toward them. As Loiperdinger and Elzer rightly pointed out, *Arrival of a Train at La Ciotat* is

> an icon of cinema's birth, rather . . . a striking example of the manipulative power allegedly inherent in cinema since its beginnings. While the fear and panic of the

audience facing Lumière's locomotive is retold in the form of an anecdote, its status reaches much higher: reiterated over and over again, it figures as the founding myth of the medium, testifying to the power of film over its spectators.[12]

Thomas Edison's production company also made many railroad-oriented films projected through his early kinetoscope, later perfecting the spectacular shock of train collisions with Edwin S. Porter's *Railroad Smash Up* (1904), "the first film to employ within a fully realized dramatic framework the characters, incidents, and settings typical of the later Western."[13] Prior to this iconic, catastrophic depiction of a head-on collision between two steam locomotives, many of Edison and Porter's films hinted at what would become Western aesthetics. *Procession of Mounted Indians and Cowboys* (1898), *Parade of Buffalo Bill's Wild West Show, No. 1* (1898) and *No. 2* (1898) depicted decorated wagons and a parade of cowboys and Indians on horseback. Edison also ventured into portraying Indigenous Americans on screen with film shorts including *Sioux Ghost Dance* (1894) and *Buffalo Dance* (1894); otherworldly and escapist, these made-for-nickelodeon shorts focused on Native Americans' tribal rituals and little else, as Alison Griffiths noted,

Thomas Edison's 1894 and 1901 actualities of Native Americans, involving several brief glimpses of Indian dances . . . invited nickelodeon audiences to don the epistemological garb of the anthropologist, witnessing the remnants of . . . indigenous life displayed in cinematic form.[14]

As Griffiths went on to assert, such naïve depictions of Indigenous Americans foregrounded an exaggerated version of the Indian commensurate with audience expectations of a "noble, savage or doomed Indian."[15] Hardly surprising then, that this early, sensational portrayal of cultural polarity—as filmicly constructed and, therefore, skewed as it was—underpinned cowboy versus Indian narratives that would define American film for generations.[16] Undoubtedly, the historical position of Native Americans on film is stereotypical and, therefore, deeply problematic. As Jacqueline Kirkpatrick stated of this misrepresentation, "The challenge presented by the 'savages' can be interpreted as a confirmation of the dominant value structure."[17] It is this aspect of the power dynamic asserted in Western film that Sioux too must have found difficult; as a persona, "Siouxsie Sioux"[18] is—*twice*—an identification with Sioux Indians as underdogs. Sioux even recalled that, "For my sixth birthday I had an Indian girl outfit and a wigwam."[19]

Edison's early films did, however, lack a central character or "hero." This critical component of Western genre was developed by Gilbert M. Anderson, otherwise known as "Broncho Billy" an actor who found his break in Porter's *Great Train Robbery* (1903) who went on to produce and star in more than three hundred Western film shorts between 1910 and 1915. By this time, the Western was a fully fledged genre. Inherently American, showcasing vast, panoramic landscapes, the foundation of the railroad, and Civil War narratives, the Western is considered by some film theorists to be "the quintessential Hollywood genre."[20]

With this in mind, "Burn-Up" can be read not only as a track that gets right to the heart of Sioux's identity, but also as the band's most cinematically realized. We can construe this from the heavily over-coded Western film music tropes inherent to the orchestration and form of "Burn-Up." As Claudia Gorbman noted, "Music is codified by the filmic context itself and assumes meaning by virtue of its placement in the film."[21] Let's consider the key dimensions of "Burn-Up" in the context of Western film.

"Burn-Up" is *Peepshow*'s most rhythmically liberated track. The slow burn of McCarrick's lengthy, introductory cello bows emulate a laboring train as it hauls itself out of a station, wheels creaking against the tracks (0.00–0.14), is a stark contrast to the densely textured final bars (3.35–end) as the train later careers out of control. While this significant tempo variation is used to successfully position the train at the epicenter of the track, this build in motion required an altogether alternate performativity, as Budgie explained

> The only truly live song on the record is Burn Up . . . we didn't even rehearse the intro. And because the song steps in its tempo in an instinctive rather than a pre-ordained way, it would have been impossible to program. So apart from a few overdubs, everything you hear is live including Siouxsie's vocal.[22]

It is not only the slow increase in tempo, but Budgie's gradual movement from whole note kick drum hits through quarters, then an eighth-note snare shuffle over the course of the introduction that, paired with the cello, perfectly simulates the locomotive. As Victor Kennedy noted, "The shuffle snare drum [is] used to evoke the image of train wheels passing over the joints in railroad tracks."[23] This technique, what Joel Dinerstein called "locomotive onomatopoeia," is as ingrained in popular music as it is in film; the aural recreation of train signifiers can be traced as far back as 1840 and is intrinsic to thousands of blues songs and jazz standards. Indeed, the "Jazz Train" and "Blues Train" styles are founded upon the locomotive, as Dinerstein suggested "the train functions as the metaphorical conveyance of choice for African American movement . . . freedom for ex-slaves: *literal* freedom."[24] The use of this rhythmic hallmark of African American music not only reinforces "Burn-Up" as a convincing slice of Americana but also ensures the aural centrality of the train at the song's core.

In 1988, such musicality could be ascribed to nostalgia, but in "Burn-Up" manifests a complex blend of historicity, film musicality, and homage. Considering *Peepshow*'s large-scale form, the juxtaposition of the liveness of "Burn-Up" between two heavily constructed album tracks pulls the record—albeit momentarily—into another direction, both in terms of musicality and history: we are in Civil War-era America, albeit a 1960s, "Spaghetti Western" interpretation of it. The New Orleans television program that inspired Sioux to write "Burn-Up" certainly grounded the track in Americana, yet the track's extraordinary sense of motion and drama owes far more to Ennio Morricone. *Once Upon a Time in the West* (1968), for example, opens with a scene of a rocking bench. Squeaking as its rusty hinges swing back and forth in the foreground, a steam train approaches, rolling into a proto-station until it grinds to a halt. Morricone's musical anchoring of Sergio Leone's iconic protagonist Harmonica with his namesake instrument elevates the score far above its traditional position as subordinate to film narrative. This use of what Royal Brown called "special instrumentation"[25] as a character-defining mechanism results in a dominant and particularly evocative score; Harmonica's identity and the sound of the instrument are inextricable. With Budgie's harmonica so prominent throughout "Burn-Up," it can, therefore, be read as a Morricone homage, particularly when situated in the context of other motifs both musical and narrative. One motif, for example, is Klein's guitar-constructed, kazoo-like gunshots that perfectly interject verse two at the point of phosphorous flying (1.10 and 1.14), as King Salamander shoots and torches his way across the land. The track also alludes to the presence of horses narratively, in the use of "giddy-up" and "blazing rubber"—presumably tires on an accompanying wagon, as well as a possible tongue-in-cheek reference to *Blazing Saddles* (1974). All these motifs in "Burn-Up" match—almost identically—the organization of music and effects in *Once Upon a Time in the West*: in the first twelve minutes of the film we hear a creaking, squeaking bench, a steam train, Harmonica playing his harmonica, and a gun fight complete with neighing horses. Budgie's harmonica in "Burn-Up" is not, however, designed as King Salamander's leitmotif. Instead, its mechanism is to create distance in an otherwise tight, up-front, and heavily textured track. The harmonica is quite probably the only overdubbed instrument in "Burn-Up." We can construe this from three factors: first, since "Burn-Up" was performed live, it would be difficult for the drums and harmonica to be performed simultaneously; secondly, the harmonica features an entirely different reverb to other instruments within the track; and, lastly, it reappears after the conclusion in an apparent musical postscript. This instrument is, therefore, detached from everything else going on and acts as a character in itself—it also fades in and out at different volumes. The form of "Burn-Up" is tightly contained and the harmonica, therefore, creates a vital sense of depth and perspective.

Morricone's ability to musically identify protagonists was matched by his construction of visually apt soundscapes augmented with musical effects, as Kenneth LeFave commented about *The Good, the Bad and the Ugly* (1966), he created

> a gritty environment of dirty, dusty danger wrapped in heatstroke . . . [translating] into orchestration the coyote calls, whistling wind, and gunshots that might inform the sound effects track of such a setting.[26]

Sioux's initial whispering vocality and the many narrative references to a sun-drenched landscape—"sun kissed," "blistered," "desert maker"—reinforce the sonic backdrop of "Burn-Up" as unforgiving wilderness and heat, mirroring Morricone's techniques. In "Burn-Up," the vocal narration begins quietly, delicately, and with a precise articulation of premonition—the "future," the murderous intention as it "ascends," the "firestarter"—all in the first three lines suggest a violent spectacle of sorts lies ahead. The later chaos and mayhem is, of course, realized in the gang vocals performed by all members of the band (3.21) as the lengthy coda speeds up until finally careering out of control. Again, the vocal performance(s) create(s) a strong contrast between the narrator's isolated position in a relatively calm wilderness at the beginning and the carnage of a speeding train, galloping horses, and gang shoot-em-up by the track's end.

Yet for all the Western motifs musically imbued in "Burn-Up," the narrative simply does not line up and, therefore, the track cannot be ascribed as simple musical appropriation of the film genre. Pramaggiore and Wallis noted two distinct types of Westerns: one where a male hero returns law and order to a community ravaged by outlaws; and, a second where a bloody war over land control erupts between cowboys and Native American Indians.[27] Narratively though, "Burn-Up" fits neither of these established Western molds. Instead, the narrator focuses on the outlaw himself, that of the pyromaniacal King Salamander and his wreaking blazing havoc across the land. On the one hand, this is a destructive, crazed arsonist intent on terror; on the other, the narrative does not pitch him against anyone else as either hero or antihero. Conversely, there is a strong sense of fun and comedic value to "Burn-Up" that suggests the narrative detail is not that serious. Severin described the track's overall aesthetic as a "hoedown"[28] (a lively folk dance) and journalists also used this term to describe "Burn-Up" at the time of *Peepshow*'s release.[29] Regardless of King Salamander's ambiguous motive, he is definitely an antihero; more a vivid premonition of a violent and destructive protagonist yet to be dreamed up by Quentin Tarantino than the charming and comparatively innocent Broncho Billy. While the story manages to weave in every fire-related signifier—firestarter, cremator, torch, burn, radiates (it's all there)—King

Salamander is ruthless, appears to have neither accomplices nor enemies, and at one point lyrically alludes to Buddy Holly/Rolling Stones hit "Not Fade Away."[30] Sioux's lead protagonist also seems related to Halloween given her analogy of King Salamander to a "Jack-O-Lantern."

"Burn-Up" is *Peepshow*'s strongest example of Siouxsie and the Banshees' songwriting strategy in narrative terms. This methodology, the situating of mythological creatures and characters as leading protagonists then conflated or analogized with contemporary narration is *Peepshow*'s hallmark: King Salamander and Rawhead and Bloodybones are two of the strongest examples; the Medusa is also alluded to later in the album in "Turn to Stone." "Burn-Up" also features a biblical reference in "fire and brimstone"[31] and the fire salamander as depicted in ancient Greece and the early twentieth-century Western, as Szientuch noted,

> In ancient Greece and Rome the salamander was believed to be a spirit that lived in the fire. Aristotle and Plynius the Elder mention a legendary lizard that dwells in the fire: the heat of the fire is neutralized by the cold of the salamander's body. Plynius the Elder, the first century AD Roman scholar of nature, reports that he tried to prove this belief experimentally—and failed: the salamander burned up.[32]

Burned up, indeed. Here, we have yet another example of Siouxsie and the Banshees' quasi-surrealist, paracinematic trademark; "Burn-Up" pushes and pulls us in opposing directions. From one angle, its musical aesthetics are firmly grounded in both Morricone's Western scores and traditional

African American musicality, yet from another, we have a narrative structure more aligned to ancient mythology than anything Sergio Leone put to film. To top it all off with yet another apparent narrative diversion, Sioux works in a nursery rhyme during the coda of "Burn-Up": "Jack be nimble, Jack be quick, Jack jump over the candlestick."[33] Or is it? In a way, this payoff line is perfect, since it conveniently packages the two main themes of the song: fire (represented by the candlestick); and, a train. For in turn-of-the-century US proto-Blues, "Jack" referred to "the locomotive—an update of its Black vernacular use for 'the indestructible donkey or jackass.'"[34] And, the position of "Burn-Up" in *Peepshow*'s large-scale form is right in the middle, at the album's core. This goes some way to explain Severin's recollection of the English record company's reception of *Peepshow* as aesthetically American, as in 1989 he said,

> And it's definitely not a particularly American album, as far as I think. But that's strange as well as our English company thinks the complete opposite: they think we've delivered an American album. Not in the terms of the material being slanted towards America but they felt that it would do well in America, which we never thought about at all![35]

Perhaps "Burn-Up" is the key to understanding how and why *Peepshow* did so well in the United States; the album's most aesthetically American track lies at its heart.

Fantasy

[CLAUDE]: You look fantastic. Like Cleopatra.
— *Eureka*

[CARMEN]: Nobody spies on me. I'm free. I'll do as
I please.
— *Carmen*

Siouxsie and the Banshees were escapists to their core. It is no surprise then that at *Peepshow*'s core lies two of the band's most other worldly, most fantastical album tracks: "Ornaments of Gold" and "Turn to Stone." The centrality of the concepts of fantasy and escapism to *Peepshow* is evident in Polydor's 1988 press kit, "The most important thing is to make your own world and atmosphere, times that take you away from the planet"[1] stated Sioux—and, arguably, the band take us furthest away in the Middle Eastern—inspired "Ornaments of Gold." In seeming contrast to this declaration of movement and change, Sioux's header quotation in *Peepshow*'s press release was a vision of monumentalism, "I can imagine myself at least 2,000 years old with banks of cats and banks of stone male statues"[2] she declared, in reference to ancient Egypt and *Peepshow*'s ode to petrification "Turn to Stone."

When considering the lyrics of "Turn to Stone," ideas of monumentalism do, however, blend with nature. For example, references to a "statue of light," the moon and tide, the chorus sea locality are good examples of Severin's trademark songwriting ambiguity. Conversely, "Ornaments of Gold" is a track dealing with luxury and opulence, the fantasy of immersing oneself in riches, all bound up in an equally heady musicality commensurate with the mythological and theological lyrical themes it draws upon. It makes sense to deal with these tracks together, because in both "Ornaments of Gold" and "Turn to Stone" we hear intoxicating blends of imagination and fantasy, which in turn create interpretive paradoxes as both tracks' musicality and narrative push and pull us in and out of histories, theologies, and mythologies.

Let's first think about both tracks in these contexts.

Mythology

"Ornaments of Gold" and "Turn to Stone" appear constructed around pillars of Greek mythology—the Midas and the Medusa respectively. In the former track, it is the intensity with which the lovers surround and "cover" themselves in gold and other riches which leads us to draw this link. King Midas, the story tells us, was granted a wish that everything he touched would turn to gold, eventually realizing his gift was in fact a curse, preventing him from eating and therefore a threat to his very existence.[3] At the heart of this ubiquitous story lies a moral code about the pursuit of immense wealth and consequences but it is also a tale of child-like fantasy, as Robert Krill noted,

> The fact that Midas acquired his treasure so effortlessly and in marked contrast to the violence so often associated with amassing it makes this story particularly well suited to the youngest readers whose imaginations are so readily drawn to beautiful things, such as the brilliant glitter of gold.[4]

A similar mythological allusion occurs in "Turn To Stone." Both the title and the song's voyeuristic theme conjures up an image of Medusa, the only mortal among three Gorgon siblings in Greek mythology and possessing the power to turn anyone looking upon her to stone. In studies on Greek mythology, Medusa is interpreted variously as "ferocious" and "erotic,"[5] and linked with the idea of transformation and abduction.[6] However, if we consider "Turn to Stone" narratively, none of these ideas really stick; the song's secondary theme of escapism diverts us from a fixed monument. To that end, while the title is undoubtedly grounded in this mythology, the music and narrative are coming from somewhere else. More likely, the song conflates the myth of Medusa with a reference to "Charon's Obol," a c. 500 BC funerary custom then-ubiquitous in the Aegean and ever-present in both Greek and Latin literature. This Greco-Roman "custom of placing a coin in the mouth of the deceased as a payment to the boatman Charon for ferrying the soul across Acheron or Styx into the underworld"[7] is referenced in "Turn to Stone": the chorus lyrics "Ferry me down" pertain to both the "ferrying" and the underworld to which ferryman Charon transported these dead bodies. Later on, we hear a reference to "fool's gold," which might be interpreted as coins.

While Greek mythology certainly underpins these two fantastic tracks, the lines between mythology and theology are blurry. "Ornaments of Gold" explicitly quotes the Koran and alludes to the Old Testament, while "Turn to Stone" refers to heaven. We'll come back to these themes in the later song analyses, but first, let's also think about how these tracks both draw on fantasy genre film tropes.

Fantasy

In his article "Fantasy, Imagination and the Screen," Robert Scruton noted the important differences between imagination and fantasy:

> In imagination, there is neither real object nor real feeling. The feeling is an imagined response to the imagined object which compels it. In fantasy there is a real feeling

which, in being prohibited, compels an unreal object for its gratification. These two phenomena, which seem on the surface to be so alike, turn out on inspection to be deeply opposed.[8]

Scruton argues that beneath all fantasy lies desire, "The desire behind fantasy is a real desire; whereas that behind imagination is not."[9] He suggests the object of desire as portrayed in film is only a surrogate for a person's true desire. I do not want to delve too deeply into psychoanalytic theory (this book does not take that approach) but it is not difficult to interpret the underlying desires in "Ornaments of Gold" and "Turn to Stone." The Sioux-penned "Ornaments of Gold" desires protection and warmth—and ultimately, security—("protect our hearts," "warm my soul") manifested in a fantasy of wealth. The Severin-authored "Turn to Stone" desires isolation ("leave well alone," "leaves us standing mute") manifested in a fantasy of petrification. But, if we consider the mythological, theological, and filmic representations of gold and monumentalism, the underlying feeling and object of gratification are always opposed. Gold, for example, does not protect; it is a material resulting from the violent means by which it has been sourced (as noted earlier by Krill), not to mention the attention it invites from—and envy it invokes in—others. Likewise, petrification does not isolate; statues result from an agreement of status and elitism. They embody iconicity and, as such, invite the communal gaze. Both these tracks are, therefore, good examples of Scruton's filmic understanding of fantasy.

In *The Fantasy Film*, Katherine Fowkes suggested "The label 'fantasy' has often been pejorative, applied to films seen to be trivial or childish or said to seduce us with unrealistic wish-fulfillment."[10] She went on to say "fantasy stories . . . feature a fundamental break with our sense of reality . . . an 'ontological rupture' is one of the hallmarks of the genre."[11] And this disruption to being, to existence, is inherent to Sioux's worldview, "To me," she said, "childhood was like [Jonathan Swift's] *Gullivers Travels,*"[12] reflecting her underlying desire to escape.

Exoticism

I want to take this opportunity to deal with a criticism that has sometimes been leveled at Siouxsie and the Banshees—that of exoticism. Throughout their career, Siouxsie and the Banshees embraced non-Western subjects and sounds. From "Hong Kong Garden" to "Arabian Knights," "Ornaments of Gold" and "Turn to Stone" could be interpreted as further examples of the band's exoticism. Timothy Taylor defined musical exoticism as "manifestations of an awareness of racial, ethnic and cultural Others captured in sound."[13] We hear these exotica as a key point of definition across Siouxsie and the Banshees' repertoire, yet their incorporation of non-Western musicality goes further than straightforward awareness or a simplistic "fetishize(d) form and style."[14] The band blends standard pop and rock forms with non-Western instrumentation, creating complex soundscapes featuring layers of both Western and non-Western progressions often in the context of the same track. To write this off as fetish or cultural appropriation would be to disavow the studied aspect of the band's sound and the various genuine—and, I would argue, successful—attempts made to assimilate non-Western aesthetics into their music. In their other band, The Creatures, Sioux, and Budgie sought to immerse themselves in the cultures of the musics they drew from: Hawai'i during the recording of *Feast* (1983), Andalucia, Spain during the sessions for the flamenco-infused *Boomerang* (1989), and their later album *Hái* (2003) was part-recorded in Japan. This immersion in global musicalities often spilled into Siouxsie and the Banshees. The band sought to be inclusive rather than simply appropriative in their non-Western influences; *Kiss Them For Me* (1992), for example, featured renowned tabla player and singer Talvin Singh who toured with the band extensively in the early 1990s. It could, therefore, be argued that Siouxsie and the Banshees' musical exotica represented the band in dialogue with the myriad global musics they encountered during the distances they travelled on tour and in which they immersed themselves. As Timothy Taylor noted in his acclaimed book *Beyond Exoticism*, we cannot consider exoticism as a "singular practice—there are, now, exoticisms"[15] and these two album tracks are certainly representational of Siouxsie and the Banshees' very nuanced exotica. Let's think about both tracks with these fantastical, mythological, theological, filmic, and exotic dimensions in mind.

Ornaments of Gold

In 1988, Sioux stated,

> That song's ["Ornaments of Gold"] about imagining adornment, intoxication. I wish people were more exotic

with one another. I was flicking through The Koran, a book there called "Ornaments Of Gold," saying "Don't look for riches on earth, you'll get them in Heaven," which is just keeping people who've got nothing content. The song's saying why not have both.[16]

In "Ornaments of Gold," Siouxsie and the Banshees construct a heavenly soundscape that references both Old Testament and Islamic ideas of heaven and the afterlife, and features distinct intertextual references to both, complete with both ascending and descending musical progressions. Temporal and spatial manipulation within the composition recreates the heady effects of wealth as Klein's guitar and McCarrick's synthesis act as embellishments, a parallel overscoring of the lover's adornment with gold ornaments as depicted in the lyrics.

Like *Peepshow* as a whole, "Ornaments of Gold" is a richly layered intertext full of cinematic influences. The direct interpolation of Koran verse melds with key themes from Nicholas Roeg's *Eureka* (1983), as Sioux stated "Yes, Eureka's a big part of it ["Ornaments of Gold"]. I love that film."[17] Roeg's film is a classic example of *film maudit*; an initially cursed, later reappraised and now canonized film. The story follows Jack McCann, who discovers a mountain of gold in the Klondike mining region of Canada. As the film progresses, McCann is gradually plagued by fear and paranoia as, overnight, he becomes the richest man in the world. The intensity with which Roeg portrays the slow constriction of wealth is mirrored in "Ornaments of Gold" lyrically, as Sioux's vocality drapes over the orchestration with a vivid imaginary of intoxication; the lyrical onomatopoeia dripping and drenching the Persian-infused musicality in glittering riches and entrancing scents.

In film history (and wider popular culture), the depiction of gold—particularly where it is plentiful—is almost always paired with death. From the deaths of Fred C. Dobbs and James Cody in *The Treasure of the Sierra Madre* (1948) to the fate of the LaHood's and Stockburn in Clint Eastwood's prospecting thriller *Pale Rider* (1985), Steyner and "Big King" in Peter R. Hunt's *Gold* (1974) to Jack McCann in *Eureka*, protagonists pay the ultimate price for their prospecting. The ways in which characters traverse this moral dichotomy of gold and death are varied, but in cinema, the dangers are foregrounded and the human cost overscored. This is also true of theological representations of gold. In the Koran, from which multiple lines are quoted, interpolated or alluded to in "Ornaments of Gold," the mercy of the Lord Allah is worth more than gold[18] (43:32) and the pursuit of gold on earth, "in the life of this world" is indicative of evil. Only those who resist wealth and the amassing of treasures will be rewarded with ornaments of gold in the afterlife (43:35),[19] as opposed to a "Punishment of Hell" (43:74).[20] Yet in "Ornaments of Gold," there is no mention of hell. There is no downfall involved in the pursuit of opulence and wealth. The track is, therefore, not just a fantasy but also a potent distillation of fantasy into its most sublime moments without the ramifications found in either *Eureka* or the Koran.

McCarrick's foregrounded (hammered) dulcimer anchors "Ornaments of Gold" in a theological musicality commensurate with the track's lyrical diegesis. The presence of the dulcimer in Western, near and Middle Eastern musical composition and performance dates back centuries; references to the stringed instrument are not found in the Koran, but in the Old Testament book of Daniel, one of six played by the Babylonians as a signal to "fall down and worship the golden image that Nebuchadnezzar the king hath set up."[21] The story is ultimately a warning against the worshipping of false Gods; Daniel's companions refused to worship Nebuchadnezzar's golden statue and as such, were thrown into a fiery furnace. The dulcimer is, however, known as a "Persian and Iraqian instrument, the name of which, *santir*, is derived from the Greek *psalterion*."[22] With immediate attacks and long, metallic decays the sound of the dulcimer—primitive in comparison to an electric guitar— conjures up a sense of mythology, an aura of the near and Middle East.

"Ornaments of Gold" marries this ancient, theologically loaded instrument with synthesized sounds and chord progressions drawn from Martin McCarrick's collection. *Peepshow* featured prominent synthesis throughout and nowhere is this more obvious than on "Ornaments of Gold." At the time, McCarrick's set up featured an Ensoniq Mirage, an 8-bit sampler synthesizer featuring an on board sequencer, an E-mu Emax sampler workstation with built-in synthesizer, an AKAI S900 sampler, a MIDI-compatible AKAI AX73 analogue synthesizer/keyboard, all controlled from a Yamaha DX-7—the defining synthesizer of the 1980s.[23] Such a rig would have given the band dozens of sounds at their fingertips, but the incorporation of so many sampling devices suggests the band were less reliant on presets and more likely to have adapted existing sounds or built their own then saved them to the various floppy drives to be controlled from the DX-7 and AX73.[24] Interestingly, the AX73 was specifically designed to synchronize with the S900 sampler, allowing users to run samples through the keyboard, and then adapt them with the AX73's filters and envelopes. At the time of production, this would have been a modest rig; the upper end of commercial pop record production was largely built around the Fairlight CMI and NED Synclavier, which were financially prohibitive. (Indeed, McCarrick's rig—featuring much cheaper and then-slightly older systems—was partially the result of economics.[25]) This instrumentation does, however, present us with the track's biggest paradox. This is a song that takes us far, far away both narratively and sonically. Yet of all *Peepshow*'s tracks, thirty years on "Ornaments Gold" is the one most tied to the era in which it was made. This is in no small part down to the extent of digital synthesis used to orchestrate it.

The entire track features heavy time-based signal processing; this deliberate distortion of temporal aspects of the musicality (aspects of the music related to time) perfectly synergizes with the track's fantasy theme. Straight away, the heavily panned introductory backward cymbal envelope with reverb suggests flight, wind, the fleeting nature of time. The aggressive spatial positioning of this introduction denotes disorientation: where—and *when*—are we? This is entirely deliberate—the intention here is to take the listener somewhere else, to transport them as far away from reality as possible. Again, lengthy reverb is present on the introductory, synthesized rhythm pattern—a loop constructed from two separate tom timbres, a heavily delayed rim shot and much quieter, yet more percussive snare. Klein's guitar underpins the dulcimer with rung-through chords, elevating it to the foreground. "Ornaments of Gold" begins as opulent and decadent, as musically indulgent as its lyrical diegesis. The draping of instruments in time-based processing, particularly: the chorused bass guitar; rich, long reverbs on a reversed synthesizer patch; and the flanging on Klein's guitar all contribute to a lush, heady soundscape. In audio engineering, applications of reverb denote an instrument as "wet"; "Ornaments of Gold" is soaked, drenched, positively *saturated* in temporal processing. This grandiose production overscores the narrative. In a passing thought at the end of his influential article on fantasy in film, Roger Scruton recognized such types of musical reinforcement,

> There is music which decks itself out in the colors of an emotion which it neither explores nor controls, but for which it provides a convenient reinforcement and perhaps a surrogate object.[26]

Let's listen to verse one (0.26–1.03). Sioux's voice is again treated with a lengthy reverb, which enhances the overall soundscape as one resembling a dream. The combination of Klein's "scaffolding" guitar, and the fleeting, sky-high spatiality with verse one's diegesis—the dancing of moon beams, the citadels, the staircase—all suggest we are far away, almost certainly high in the sky. Lyrically, explicit references are made to the light "below" and "ascending" stairs thus reinforcing an image of height, of elevation.

The foregrounding of McCarrick's dulcimer also places the orchestration far back in time. Further temporal distortion features on "surrounded" (0.41–0.43), with a reversed reverb envelope preceding the line. The significant alliteration in this line is underscored with ethereal synth chords, floating along Severin's heavily chorused, staccato bass. At the last line of verse one (0.50–0.58), the combination of "Eureka"— the name of Jack McCann's luxurious Caribbean estate—with an "angelic prayer" poeticizes the Islamic promise of riches in the afterlife. This prayer is underscored with an ethereal, cascading synth arpeggio emulating sparkling, shining lights. With this carefully orchestrated soundscape featuring a biblical instrument, as well as an opulent lyrical diegesis focused on height—the first two lines are identical to those featured in the Koran—there is no doubt we are being drawn into Siouxsie and the Banshees' idea of heaven, of the afterlife.

Until now, Klein's metamorphic guitar and Severin's chorused bass meld with the synth lines in a cohesive soundscape. Reinforced by the production with a jump in loudness simultaneous to Budgie's snare roll, Klein's distorted guitar and Budgie's drums enter at the first chorus, which disrupts this soundscape as if signifying a reality check. At this point in the track—in fact, at this point on *Peepshow*—Klein's guitar is at its straightest, typically "rock" sound. Percussive synth chords (these are the only sounds that resemble DX-7 presets) divert from the constant kick drum rhythm, positioned high in the mix above the background drum loop. Again, Budgie's cymbals are positioned particularly high in the mix on "gold" (1.03), "cold" (1.11), "gold" (1.19), and then at 1.27 as a short break moves into verse two.

Group backing vocals feature throughout the chorus (1.04–1.07; 1.12–1.15), which have not been treated in the same way as the lead vocal. (Incidentally, these lines are omitted from the lyric sheets in the CD and vinyl releases.) They feature as a chorus choir, appear slightly pitched up, and are processed with a lengthy reverb. Sioux's voice definitely features in this chorus; we hear it emerge from these group backing vocals into lead lines. It is, however, cohesively melded with Severin and/or McCarrick's vocal, precisely in time and heavily processed so as to form a chorus. A backward reverb circles around these group vocals as if they are coming from somewhere else entirely: airy and celestial, they signify voices from another world and could be read as angels.

If the first verse signified ascent, the second verse contrasts this with a clear musical descent. Orchestration-wise, verse two is more complex, featuring a continuum of the sharp, percussive chorus synth stabs in a descending semi-tone, which pulls the track downward. Interestingly, the lyrics match this apparent downscaling: in the Koran, verse 43:63 states,

> Enter Paradise, you and your spouses, in all delight.
> You shall be served with golden dishes and golden cups.[27]

Yet in "Ornaments of Gold," the allusion is to *silver* vessels and bowls. This presents a marked shift in intertextual form, since we've moved from direct quotation and interpolation in verse one to a more complex allusion in verse two.

Budgie's kick drum powers through, but it is Severin's augmenting of McCarrick's descending chords with the bass (1.27–1.40), which promptly breaks into eighth-notes and continues on this descending trajectory, that completes this verse as a downward spiral (1.40–1.47). This ascent/descent contrast pushes and pulls the two verses in opposing directions, as McCarrick suggested,

> We're not just rooting the chords all the time . . . we worked to make the most of that, to put a bit more pushing and pulling in the music. Listen to the second verse of "Ornaments Of Gold" and you'll hear what I mean. The chord stays the same all the way but the base of the music is moving down in semi tones, semi-resolving all the time, which gives a subtle jarring feel.[28]

That this descent ends on "intoxicating oils" is not a coincidence. Sioux told of her admiration of soundscapes that transcended reality and at this point in the track, she alludes to this heavenly dream world as one induced by drugs. This is precisely how she analogized Nicolas Roeg's cinematography in Eureka,

> Nic Roeg's camera work trips! It really does what you can do either by day dreaming or under the influence of something—it makes things change as you're thinking about them. You wonder if he'd fed his camera LSD or something.[29]

Fantasizing or intoxicated? Either way, we are far away from reality and the opulence of the music itself mirrors the lyrical preoccupation with riches. And this is how we are to perceive the consumption of infinite riches: in verse one, this is a heavenly ascent, by verse two, a similar narrative underscored by a musical descent acts as the only presence of warning, of consequence in the entire track.

The last two lines of verse two are the most embellished, both musically and lyrically (1.48–2.08). Here, we hear Budgie's cymbals overscoring the opulence on "drenched" and "unimaginable," as well as the fleeting return of the cascading "angelic prayer" synth line from verse one on "jewels."

By the second chorus, the layered orchestration results in a richly textured soundscape made busier by Budgie's tom fills; this pushes "Ornaments of Gold" into its most percussive section—the underlying loop is still present. Klein's guitar begins to overlay this densely percussive chorus with classic rock interjections, almost metal-like in their tonality and phrasing. Consider the guitar at 2.20 as it traverses a three-note crescendo; this is *Peepshow*'s only allusion to classic rock, disappearing as quickly as it arrives. The guitar's mechanism is one that underscores distance: its function is to denote the vast distances present between reality and fantasy in the song, but on a macro level, the fleeting, almost desperate way in which the guitar briefly features, signifies the musical distance between Siouxsie and the Banshees and wider classic rock of the era.

No sooner are we lulled into a percussion break that Severin's spinning bass guitar draws us back into this heady affair (2.33). A middle eight vocal break reinforces this song as fantasy: let's not forget that this narrative is not an experiential one. McCarrick's fleeting, upper register synth lines augment this daze (2.37–2.45), embellishing the fantasy with an aural construction of jewelry, glimmering top notes that mirror the lyrics. By the third chorus, the backing vocals linger on the imagined ornaments as Klein's guitar dive bombs (2.55), again referencing a classic rock trope. At this point, the song is turned around; at 3.01, Klein's foregrounded guitar performs a dramatic ascent, before reaching a plateau. There is a sense of struggle between the guitar and percussion in this final chorus and coda, as if the guitar is fighting for its place. This tension between the two instruments does, however, align with the recording process. Sioux rearranged "Ornaments of Gold" between the pre-production sessions at Ardingly and the recording sessions at Marcus studios and, as McCarrick recalled, "Siouxsie took it [the backing track] home, re-wrote the lyrics, got rid of all the music and completely re-constructed the whole song using a drumbox and a vocal."[30] The result is a song focused on drums and percussion with the guitar and keyboards added for effect, for embellishment. We hear further examples of this at 3.20 with a delayed, sharp pinch harmonic and at 3.28 an upward bend resulting in a squeal; once again, these are traditional, classic rock guitar techniques featured here as effects and almost in competition with the synthesis. During the coda, the rhythm guitar also features a flanger, which swirls around the backing vocals in a densely textured stupor.

Siouxsie and the Banshees' "Ornaments of Gold" basks in the wealth and luxury of gold without any of the moral baggage normatively associated with the depiction of plentiful gold in mythology, theology, or on film. It is pure escapist fantasy removed from the darker implications of the inevitable return to reality.

Turn to Stone

"Turn to Stone" is one of the more complicated and multifaceted tracks on *Peepshow* that can be read and interpreted on multiple levels. In saying that its central petrification fantasy is explicitly embodied in the title and chorus; this is a realization of monumentalism, which is further reinforced with narrative of "marble" and a "statue." There is, however, a paradox in "Turn to Stone," since this fantasized monumentalism occurs against a flowing flamenco backdrop. How the lyrical themes drawn from Greco-Roman mythology and theology reconcile with this Spanish music and dance tradition is possibly *Peepshow*'s most challenging question, but this twisting and turning of European traditions and histories certainly reinforces the album's overall *Caligarisme* aesthetic.

One underlying reason for this move into flamenco is the band's admiration of Spanish film and Spain in general. Post-*Peepshow*, Sioux and Budgie were based in Spain during the recording of The Creatures' *Boomerang* and, as Budgie stated, "We had always been aware of Spanish film directors, versions of Carmen and the power of the Flamencan dance troupes— the brilliant syncopation of the beat, the clapping."[31]

Budgie also spoke of the band's appreciation of Spanish cinema, particularly versions of Bizet's famous opera *Carmen*. One key version of the film by Carlos Suara, the Academy award-nominated *Carmen* (1983), features a theatrical interpretation of Bizet's famous opera. Suara's film follows Antonio, a lead choreographer, and Carmen, a young flamenco dancer as she auditions for a dance work based on Bizet's original opera. Like Bizet's tragic character Antonio, the film's Antonio falls in love with Carmen, and the most significant aspect of the film is the way the lovers traverse their personal relationship in parallel to the story-within-a-story version of the opera as played out through a highly choreographed dance work. By the end of the film, their personal lives and dance climax are inextricable as Antonio kills Carmen in a fit of jealous rage. The flamenco portrayed throughout Suara's film is upbeat, rowdy and densely textured with percussive layers of dance steps and castanets—a depiction of flamboyance and passion inherent to the flamenco tradition.

While "Turn to Stone" features a much slower, delicate flamenco than that in Suara's *Carmen*, the passion and sensuality is captured both musically in Klein's understated Spanish guitar and Budgie and Severin's triplet-based rhythms, and narratively in Severin's lyrics. Words including the moon (and implied moonlight), glowing, pulsating, swooning, heaven, swims (and implied swimming), all evoke passionate, and sensual movement in less a direct appropriation of flamenco form and more a fantasized flamenco soundscape. Of all the album tracks on *Peepshow*, "Turn to Stone" is of the more musically straightforward, yet lyrically and conceptually complicated. Multiple aspects of this moderate, flamencan fantasy simply do not line up; there is a discontinuity between this fantasy of monumentalism in all its cold rigidity on the one hand and the sensual, balmy warmth of passionate Spanish flamenco on the other. This lack of cohesion between music and lyrics reinforces a dream-like soundscape as heady and as intoxicating as "Ornaments of Gold."

The introduction of "Turn to Stone" is not dissimilar to that of "Ornaments of Gold" in that it evokes flight. The notion of fantasy is again denoted by the temporal distortions present: the whiplash-style percussion samples against two-note bongo progressions, underpinned with high-pitched, swelling analogue synth chords (we can hear this from the noise and hiss attached to the sounds—turn the introduction up and you'll hear it) and a much sharper, low frequency-heavy synth with an unnaturally truncated decay, push and pull this *concréte*-style introduction in opposing directions. This experimental sound collage is drawn more from the mid-twentieth-century radiophonic workshops and the minimalist canon than any popular music of the era. Again, this foregrounds *Peepshow*'s *Caligarisme*.

By 0.19, Sioux's vocal introduction emerges from this collage; a sample loop formed from a tiny, repeated snippet of the introductory word "high" and slowly increasing in volume until flowing into the opening line. This creates an effective sense of approach; the voice seems far away before slowly appearing in the foreground. Just like "Ornaments of Gold," this constructive musicality is designed to reinforce distance. By 0.24, we are suddenly propelled from this experimental soundscape into the flamenco; all aspects of the initial analogue synthesis and samples immediately disappear. It's as if we've fallen into a time warp and come out the other side. This surrealist transmogrification is further disoriented (if that is possible) by the narrative. Musically, Budgie's syncopated drum rhythm and Klein's rung-through acoustic guitar chords over Severin's triplet bass line create the flamenco canvas, positioning the track in Spain but just like in "Ornaments of Gold," we are somewhere "high above." A further disorienting factor lies in the "sickle moon"; this evocative sickle image evokes both the crescent moon of Islam and the flag of the Soviet Union and communism. In a further contradiction, verse one references to drowning and the tide suggest being pulled under the sea. These are the extremities of our world, vast distances that most of us can only imagine; "Turn to Stone" is ambitious in its attempt to traverse these extreme highs and lows. Yet this could well be the key to the whole song; the navigation from above the moon to beneath the sea analogizing the distance between sensual closeness (in the flamenco underscore) and isolated separation (in the title and chorus narrative).

The sampled vocal loop technique is used again on the second line beginning "all" (0.28) and on the fourth "reaction" (0.45). A much softer lead-in occurs at 0.52 prior to the chorus, which features a foregrounded eighth-note synth melody, jarring against Budgie and Severin's flamenco groove. The prominent "ferry" is a natural chorus continuation of the tide in verse one; we are traversing a fantasy world by sea. Yet there is a darkness to the chorus, a warning to be left alone. This musicality reinforces the song as inspired at least in part by Charon's Obol, which, as Susan Stevens suggested, represented a much broader funerary practice across the Greco-Roman and near-Eastern world involving coins and the ferrying of bodies out to sea.[32] Fittingly, then, the chorus takes a darker musical turn reflecting this death custom.

No sooner do we perceive "Turn to Stone" as a song of isolation—and probably of death—that another protagonist, a "guest," is introduced in verse two. Despite the introductory sample loops on "here" (from 1.16) and "far" (1.32), verse two is delivered from a different space entirely. The vocals are whispered, softly sung and spoken, treated with a lengthy reverb that underscores the narrative of a phantom's presence, again aligning with the death theme in Charon's Obol. This verse juxtaposes with verse one, which narrates an external, upward and outward environment. By verse two, this is flipped around; the protagonist focuses on the "here," the internal and inside (1.36)—the application of this heavy reverb suggests these are thoughts, imaginings in contrast to the fantasies evoked in verse one. Despite the apparently welcome presence of this guest, there is no interaction; whether that's because the guest is a phantom, a figment of the protagonist's imagination (likely) or a real figure our lead protagonist simply does not want to interact with is ambiguous. Either way, this verse, which also features Klein's guitar breaking into flamenco-style arpeggios, has softened the harsh rigidity of chorus monumentalism.

A metallic, percussive, almost industrial loop is introduced in the second chorus (1.51), its timbre incongruently jarring against the seductive, flamencan verse. At this point, the timbral contrast between verses and choruses appear to denote the differences in the protagonists (external) environment and (internal) emotion: the former appearing sublime, calm and beautiful, the latter apparently frozen, monumental. This dissonant loop is foregrounded (2.08–2.15) before a middle eight, featuring a prominent vocal cry that blends fantasized environment (heaven) with reference to both fool's gold and marble (2.28), another monumental reference.

Aside from the introduction sample loop on "high" (2.28), the final verse is left comparatively dry. Like the middle eight, this final verse musically and lyrically blends the dreamy environment with emotive expression while simultaneously distorting place and time. In verse one, the imagined place and time is out of mind (0.43); this time, they are out of sight (2.50). This suggests that, somewhere along this fantastic journey, the protagonist has experienced the initially imagined environment. There is, however, a final fantasy in this extraordinary world and it is one of hope that somehow, stone monuments, statues may be brought to life (2.55–3.01). This is the most convincing indication yet that we are dealing with stone and monumentalism as a metaphor for emotion, that distances between people may be traversed, that cold, mute emotions may be awakened.

Yet following a double chorus, the 40-second long coda finishes the track as it begins, foregrounding the sharp synth chords, this time in tandem with the industrial loop. This is a stark, soulless finale to an overall warm and sensuous track. By the conclusion, a dense reverb is wound in to Budgie's final percussion hits as the initial drum loop fades; the song has traversed a full circle.

"Turn to Stone" is a good example of the sampler used as an instrument, to create original sounds and textures rather than quote from existing sources. While the vocal lead-in sample loops were quite probably created in McCarrick's rig, further manipulation has occurred in the studio, since there are further time-based signal processing and volume manipulations present. There is no doubt that "Turn to

Stone" implements the most "studio constructivist" approach of all *Peepshow*'s tracks.

Overall, both "Ornaments of Gold" and "Turn to Stone" represent Siouxsie and the Banshees' escapism, both musically and lyrically. The continental European and near-Eastern influences in both tracks create exotic musical canvases upon which conflations of mythological, theological and filmic narration are painted. Both tracks also illustrate the band's extraordinary depth of artistic inspiration, not to mention knowledge of the humanities, particularly classics, literature and theology. Critically, both songs also reflect the band's ability to create complex, micro-detailed soundscapes befitting of macro themes, to weave textures and timbres effortlessly in and out of multidimensional narratives. This methodology reflects fantasy cinema. At its very best.

Horror

[CAROL ANNE] They're here.
— *Poltergeist*

[MARIA] Who are you? I'm Maria. Will you play with me?
Would you like one of my flowers?
— *Frankenstein*

[DOLL MAKER] This doll had almost been loved to death.
You know, love inflicts the most terrible injuries on my
small patients.
— *Bunny Lake Is Missing*

Siouxsie and the Banshees' affinity with horror film is inextricable from their music. Often, journalists missed the opportunity to explore this in depth, instead ascribing superficial similarities to Hammer Horror films and Hitchcock. While Sioux stated her "favorite films"[1] were those of the Hammer Company, the depth of horror influence present in the Banshees' lyrics and musicality cannot be ascribed to this single filmic dimension. There are obvious references to Hitchcock in tracks such as "Spellbound"[2] and the horror of child abuse is addressed directly in both "Playground Twist"[3] and "Candyman"[4] but *Peepshow* features a more accomplished, nuanced horror track in the form of "Rawhead and Bloodybones," as Sioux stated about the influence of horror on the band generally,

> We are talking about horror in the broadest sense . . . so it could include something like incest. Otherwise it degenerates into a generalisation I don't like about the Banshees and that's horror in the narrow sense of schlock, eyeballs, brains, the offal factor . . .[5]

George Pavlou's 1986 adaptation of Clive Barker's *Rawhead Rex* (1984)[6] was more a homage to Edward D. Wood's 1950s sci-fi horror B movies than a recreation of the original monster as depicted in folklore. While *Rawhead Rex* features all the paracinematic clichés of low budget B movies made by Hammer and AIP, this was not the inspirational trigger for "Rawhead and Bloodybones," despite the proximity of the film's release to *Peepshow*'s production sessions. Sioux attributed the origin of "Rawhead" to a book Budgie was reading on

Celtic legends;[7] the tale of Rawhead and Bloodybones can be traced back nearly five centuries.[8]

As Archer Taylor described in *The Journal of American Folklore*, Raw Head and Bloody Bones is a specter—a gruesome, imaginary figure used to frighten children into obedience.[9] Although Taylor suspected "no traditional story about it ever existed"[10] he suggested that over centuries, tales of Rawhead and Bloodybones evolved to become a mainstay of British and American folklore. By the turn of the twentieth century, the monster was associated with water; Eliza Gutch described Rawhead as "a kind of ghost that haunts wells"[11] and Elizabeth Wright suggested Rawhead was "a masculine water demon."[12] More recently, Ruth Tongue described Bloody Bones as living "in a dark cupboard, usually under the stairs."[13] Yet an American variation on the tale describes Rawhead and Bloodybones as a hog, a friend of a woman named Old Betty. After Rawhead is slaughtered and hung up for gutting, Old Betty attempts to bring him back to life with a chant, and as Schlosser describes

> the bloody bones reassembled themselves into the skeleton of a razorback hog . . . The head hopped on top of his skeleton . . . He borrowed the sharp teeth of a dying panther, the claws of a long-dead bear, and the tail from a rotting raccoon.[14]

Although the lyrical narrative in "Rawhead and Bloodybones" alludes to both Wright and Tongue's understanding of the specter, it is this American depiction of Rawhead and Bloodybones that Sioux explicitly refers to in verse four. However, while lyrically acknowledging its historicity, the predicament of the narrator is drawn from classic, contemporary horror film tropes.

"Rawhead and Bloodybones" narrative relies on the relationship between Sioux's child protagonist and Rawhead and Bloodybones as a (imagined?) monster and as such, features a number of child-oriented motifs. In film, the aural and visual placement of baby and child-related signifiers to exacerbate fear—lullabies, nursery rhymes, music boxes, babies crying, children's laughter, fairground music, and the like—never fails to invoke anxiety in even the most hardened horror fans. In his chapter, "The Monster and the Music Box: Children and the Soundtrack of Horror," Stan Link suggests that "the 'innocent' tune and its musical antithesis, although found in any cinematic genre, becomes doubly effective in horror, and redoubled by interplay with children."[15] I would go further and suggest the impact is redoubled again when the child is female. There is a reason why the protagonists of Wes Craven's benchmark slasher film *Nightmare on Elm Street* were children: being slashed to death by Freddy Krueger's razor blade glove is one thing; that this horrific imaginary is conjured up in the dreams of sixteen-year-old Nancy Thompson, one of cinema's most sophisticated and lauded female child protagonists,[16] is quite another. The younger the child, the greater their vulnerability and, therefore, more horrific the effect—the relentless anxiety instilled in the viewer throughout Tobe Hooper and Steven Spielberg's *Poltergeist* is largely because Carol Anne is a five-year-old girl. From the Grady twins in Stanley Kubrick's *The Shining* to the possessed Damien in Richard Donner's *The Omen*, the child-in-peril or child-possessed is horror cinema's lynchpin. More nuanced is the relationship between the monster and the child. In some cases, including *Poltergeist*, the monster is less a visible character and more an antagonist manifestation of projected fear—just like Rawhead and Bloodybones. In these cases, we as an audience helplessly look on while, despite the unfolding horror, our protagonist appears to empathize with their tormentor, as Linda Williams suggested,

> The strange sympathy and affinity that often develops between the monster and the girl may thus be less an expression of sexual desire (as in King Kong, Beauty and the Beast) and more a flash of sympathetic identification.[17]

The relationship between Frankenstein's monster and Maria in James Whale's *Frankenstein* (1931) epitomizes this connection. The iconic pond scene where the two unlikely friends bond was so disturbing, it was originally deemed too horrifying by Universal Pictures, who cut it, as Richard Anobile stated,

> The original scene did not end with the monster motioning to the girl but continued as he tossed her into the pond, thinking she would float like the daisies. The girl screams and slowly sinks beneath the surface of the water. The monster, confused and disappointed, leaves.[18]

Another variation on the child/monster trope is found in Fritz Lang's 1931 benchmark proto-noir *M* (1931). Here, the cinematographic focus is not so much on the child, but on the *absence* of the child. A balloon floating off into telephone lines, a ball rolling away onto the grass, a sweet wrapper, as well as a group of children reciting a playground rhyme all evoke Elsie's absence as opposed to her presence. That Hans Beckert the child killer's leitmotif is the childish, mischievous lead melody from Edvard Greig's *In The Hall of the Mountain King* only intensifies the sense of urgency with which he must be captured.

A key feature of "Rawhead and Bloodybones" is the disturbing metamorphosis of Sioux's voice so as it resembles the child protagonist. Again, this is a mechanism drawn from a horror film and not from popular music. In EMP's 2016 exhibition, *Can't Look Away: The Lure of Horror Film*, composer Steve Fisk stated, "Few things are more disconcerting than the wrong sound coming out of someone's mouth"[19] in reference to metamorphoses of voice in films such as William Friedken's *The Exorcist* (1973). The demonically possessed Regan MacNeil is horror cinema's most extreme example, but similar terror is invoked where the vocal metamorphosis is more nuanced. For example, in an iconic scene from *The Shining* (1980), Danny Torrance is possessed by his imaginary friend Tony and croaks out "redrum" while running his fingers down the blade of a carving knife as his mother sleeps.

"Rawhead and Bloodybones" key musical feature is Jon Klein's guitar emulation of a music box. Again, this is another cinematic motif representing age, innocence, and regression. Such a trope conjures up sinister connotations in *Night of the Living Dead* (1968). Through a peephole *vignette* we see Barbara slowly exploring a long-abandoned room as taut, anticipatory strings are augmented with an ascending xylophone motif. As Barbara approaches a music box, its mirrored panels unfold revealing her fractured face. Indeed, this ubiquitous horror trope was pioneered by Bernard Herrmann, as Howard Goodall noted, "Hermann knew that by using sounds associated with a children's nursery, he could indicate subliminally to the listener the idea of a haunted past or ruined innocence."[20]

What we have in "Rawhead and Bloodybones" then is a sophisticated conflation of a story anchored in folklore, reinforced with musical motifs drawn from a contemporary horror film and film music. The music box, the young female child protagonist, a mildly empathetic relationship with a monster, a regressive metamorphosis of voice and, significantly, a hiding place, are all bound up in this extraordinary reflection of childhood fear.

"Rawhead and Bloodybones" features Jon Klein's most significant contribution to *Peepshow*. The immediacy of his heavily chorused guitar-as-music-box creates a creepy, yet contained atmosphere for *Peepshow*'s shortest, most unsettling track. Klein's guitar rig featured multiple vintage pedals, including plenty of modulation such as the Morley Auto Flange and Electro Harmonix effects.[21] Used in conjunction with the Eventide Harmonizer in Marcus Studios,[22] an almost infinite range of possible sound effects was well within reach of the band—particularly Sioux, who throughout her career pursued a non-guitar guitar sound. Klein's music box melody oscillates between heavily modulated and comparatively clean settings throughout resulting in a playful, childish backdrop; Klein even described his Coloursound Dipthonizer pedal as similar in sound to "that kids' cartoon Roobarb and Custard."[23] While Klein's guitar emulates a classic music box horror trope, the soundscape is created from the vocal and cello, as well as the production.

In *The Monstrous-Feminine*, Barbara Creed suggested,

> Almost a cliché of the contemporary horror film is the scene where the hunted locks her/himself inside the room, trunk or cupboard and waits, hardly daring to breathe, as the killer tries to force an entry. The victim huddles in a foetal position as if trying to disappear into the walls.[24]

In this track, we hear Sioux narrating the tale of "Rawhead and Bloodybones" from the very environments described in folklore as Rawhead's hiding places. The regressive metamorphosis of Sioux's voice in "Rawhead" is deliberately constructed around a monosyllabic delivery. Here, the main protagonist is a small, frightened young girl narrating an abridged version of the story from a first-person perspective. The voice—although clear and up front in the mix—is heavily processed with multiple time-based signal processors: the voice features a lengthy pre-delay,[25] a further short delay as well as a large reverb with a blunt decay time. The combination of these effects in verse one (0.12–0.33) fabricates a small, contained space—the cupboard—from which Sioux's frightened young girl persona narrates. This claustrophobic space is intensified by the excessively foregrounded vocal in much the same way as close-up shots on actors' faces in cinema; these techniques are designed to bring the listener (or viewer, as in film) as close as possible to the protagonist. This technique is found in Otto Preminger's thriller *Bunny Lake Is Missing* (1965), a film based around the ambiguous world of incestuous siblings. A key scene depicts extreme close-up shots of lead character Ann Lake as she slowly climbs the stairs of the nursery school from where her daughter Bunny has disappeared. When Ann finds an old man fixing broken dolls in the dark nursery attic, this technique not only brings the viewer much closer to her desperation but also significantly contracts the space she inhabits. As Mary Anne Doane suggested,

> The camera moves to follow her trajectory, but at points she approaches the camera so closely that the image becomes quasi-abstract . . . an excessive proximity that produces at least a transitory illegibility and disorientation, witnessed by the broken dolls, fragmented simulacra of discarded human bodies.[26]

This notion of excessive proximity can be heard throughout "Rawhead and Bloodybones," particularly in verse one and two's fabrication of the cupboard space. At the turn of verse three, however, the claustrophobic cupboard location changes.

The appearance of a prominent, synthesized wind instrument, likely a bass recorder, reinforces this as the perspective of a child. The chorus effect returns to the guitar after the word "pond" (0.55) and modulation is added to the vocal on the word "well" (0.58); here, the heavily processed guitar and voice embodies meaning; these production aesthetics aurally construct a body of water, which explicitly mirrors the lyrical references. In verse three, the protagonist and others are "down here" (1.03), presumably in the bottom of the well. Here, the modulated delay effect applied to the voice is manually increased as the verse narrative progresses; the prominent, delayed oscillations simulate their "drowning" in the well.

"Rawhead," therefore, features accurate constructions of both the cupboard and well as depicted in traditional folklore, but the track works on multiple levels. Let's listen to the introduction and first verse again, this time focusing on Martin McCarrick's cello. This instrument is processed entirely differently to the guitar and voice and features a lengthy reverb. Its lower position in the mix relative to the voice and guitar and center-left position in the stereo field situates it far off, outside the cupboard and well. McCarrick uses two distinctive cello motifs throughout "Rawhead": the first is a descending glissando evoking sadness or crying; the second are sporadic, discordant scrapes that emulate a rusty swing or see saw. The juxtaposition of Sioux's claustrophobic vocal with McCarrick's distant, reverberant cello therefore creates multiple spaces within the same track: one for the narrator and one for Rawhead, or, where the narrator imagines Rawhead to be. In mimicking playground sounds, the cello signifies the child's *absence* from the space they should be in a similar construction to that in *M* and *Bunny Lake Is Missing*. In the opening scene of the latter film, for example, protagonist Steven Lake walks across the back garden to his home, pausing as a squeaky swing—rocking backward and forward as though only recently vacated—is positioned in the foreground of this shot, denoting the absence of the child. In "Rawhead and Bloodybones" McCarrick's cello works in exactly this way.

In contrast to most of *Peepshow*'s heavily textured percussion, Budgie's addition of classic, spine-tingling triangle appears only in the vocal breaks. Following verse four, a couple of tiny, yet heavily reverberant triangle hits appear to evoke the sound of stones being dropped in a well thus reinforcing the position of the narrator (1.48–1.54).

With Sioux's vocal so prominent in this mix, it would be easy to conclude she is crouched in this hiding place alone. But she isn't. Background voices add another layer of functionality, appearing momentarily in verse one (0.34–0.38) then reappearing (0.56), for the duration of verse two and throughout the remainder of the track. This is no coincidence, since it is at this point that Sioux indicates the presence of others by using the pronouns "we" and "we're." However, unlike Sioux's lead vocals, these background voices are indecipherable, distant, and unplaceable and are indicative of what Michel Chion termed an *acousmêtre*: "A kind of voice-character specific to cinema that in most instances of cinematic narratives derives mysterious powers from being heard and not seen."[27] The presence of these acousmatic voices is never resolved: there is no direct interaction between them and the lead protagonist.

Sioux's child-like performativity is augmented at the very end of the track, where the sound of an even younger child crying is wound in to the mix; tears merge with Klein's spiraling guitar as the recorder melody breaks down until all that is left is a reverberant wash. What we have here is a track that not only depicts contemporary horror tropes, but one that is acutely aware of its historicity: this conflation of children and fright in horror did not originate with *The*

Exorcist or *The Omen*. Here, the Banshees take a ubiquitous film trope and reframe it at its very origin.

On the matter of large-scale form, simply put, *Peepshow* would not work as well as it does without "Rawhead" in this precise location. Second only to "Peek-A-Boo," "Rawhead" is the most important track on the album, since its short length and minimalist structure is a barrier mechanism that breaks the album's musical flow. For "Rawhead and Bloodybones" is a reflective track as well as a regressive one and absorbs us listeners into an imaginary, yet disturbing scenario before *Peepshow*'s climactic, *epic* finale.

Epic

[SCARLETT]: When the war is over, Ashley.
When the war is over.
— *Gone with the Wind*

[NARRATOR]: And then the cannons of the Battleship
open fire in retaliation against the savagery of the armed
forces of Odessa.
— *The Battleship Potemkin*

Peepshow's encore is an inherently epic one. Its conceptual basis is nailed firmly to the mast of drama; its two-song, ten-minute trajectory simultaneously demonstrates a command of gentle and understated musicality, and intense, symphonic crescendo. No wonder then that *Peepshow*'s dramatic climax is also its most explicitly filmic; no musical expense is spared as "The Last Beat of My Heart" and "Rhapsody" draw heavily on the ultimate in cinematic achievement: the epic.

In film, the epic is a much-debated genre of "grandiose visions";[1] epic cinema represents an excessive realization of love, war, and other landmark historical events. Epic is, as media theorist Vivian Sobchack put it, an "extravagant generality and excess—of sets, costumes, stars, and spectacle, of the money and labor that went into the making of such entertainment."[2] In many cases, this approach to filmmaking results in the elevation of the immense technological and personnel effort inherent to the production above the narrative itself.

From a musicological angle, it makes sense to consider *Peepshow*'s final two tracks "The Last Beat of My Heart" and "Rhapsody" together since they both play out on vast, war-torn stages and, each track is essentially a tale of survival. Drawing on Severin's thoughts of "Europe on the cusp of World War I,"[3] both songs evoke the mood of this sprawling historical era, yet also reference the conscious physicality of survival in a human sense: the lovers "dare to breathe" in "The Last Beat of My Heart," while in "Rhapsody," both protagonists are "breathing in air drunk dry." This lends both tracks a dramatic sense of scale, of great wars conquered paired with the profound realization of existence on an individual level. Additionally, both songs evoke epic film in its traditional sense; particularly the historical wartime spectacle featuring what Tom Brown called "the décor of history" (historical verisimilitude) as "an excess of detail"[4] and "the spectacular vista" (settings and views of grand scale) as "an excess of action."[5] In the case of these tracks, "The Last Beat of My Heart," unravels in a ravaged environment indicative of a spectacular vista; by contrast, "Rhapsody" is specifically staged in the Stalin-era Soviet Union and reflects this décor of history. These two immense tracks carry the musical as well as narrative aesthetics of epic; prominent in *Peepshow*'s dramatic coda is Sioux and Severin's deep love of classical music. The ambitious, symphonic nature of the compositions, heavily textured orchestration, and Sioux's commanding vocality demonstrate more in common with modernist classical music, than perhaps even the pop or rock of the era.

Sioux and Severin's writing approach to "The Last Beat of My Heart" and "Rhapsody" is indicative of what Tom Brown called "the historical gaze":[6] an articulation of "the film character's relationship to the history of which he or she is a part"[7] and a key trope in epic film genre, since it deals with the character's negotiation of history. At the point of *Peepshow*, Sioux and Severin's historical gaze was already well crafted. Consider Sioux's take on "Cities in Dust," for example, taken from the band's 1986 album *Tinderbox* and inspired by the petrification of the city of Pompeii:

> Seeing a whole civilization petrified in lava was like putting yourself in the place at the time. . . . I find it really

easy to do that, to get ghost images of life continuing as it was. I often wonder if that's what real hauntings are—your imagination and your senses bringing things back to life. That's why you'd never be able to capture it on film.[8]

Just like a film character, Sioux imagines herself in this place, at this particular point in time, yet concludes the insurmountable challenge of portraying such an event on film. This classic example of Sioux and Severin's historical gaze in songwriting is sharpened in "The Last Beat of My Heart"; a commanding love song playing out on an epic stage. Let's consider this track first. A classic "Till Death us do Part" story is told entirely from Sioux's perspective. There are no defined characters. No creatures from folklore or mythology. And, in stark contrast to the ambiguity present throughout *Peepshow*'s diegeses to this point, "The Last Beat of My Heart" is comparatively straightforward. Lyrically, this song features more "my" and "I" than the rest of *Peepshow* put together as it earnestly articulates the aching and yearning of a love torn apart. Quite fittingly, this love is never united, resolved, concluded, or otherwise satisfied. That it leaves the listener hanging with such melancholy is part of its endurance, its timelessness. "The Last Beat of My Heart" was the third and final of *Peepshow*'s singles, a Christmas release at the end of 1988, yet in only reaching number forty-four in the UK chart, fell far short of the hit single mark (likely due to the commercial dominance of an emergent house coupled with Stock Aitken and Waterman's utilitarian hit factory).

While epic films feature many common threads, including the excesses previously mentioned by Tom Brown, broader subgenre aesthetics are often weaved in to the narrative and *mise en scène*, such as romance or Western. Consider Sioux's description of "Something Blue," B-Side of "The Passenger" (1986): "My romantic notions were of the cinematic and epic proportion."[9] In "The Last Beat of My Heart" Sioux and Severin draw heavily upon the romance, or, more specifically, the *melodrama* as a facet of epic and it is through this filmic lens that "The Last Beat of My Heart" makes the most sense.

Melodrama and "The Last Beat of My Heart"

In *Melodrama Revised*, Linda Williams stated,

> Melodrama is the fundamental mode of popular American moving pictures . . . that seeks dramatic revelation of moral and emotional truths through a dialectic of pathos and action. It is the foundation of the classical Hollywood movie.[10]

"The Last Beat of My Heart" is, of course, imbued with this potent blend of pathos and action; the heart-wrenching lyrics simultaneously refer to the melancholy of love torn apart as well as an explicit reference to a "war-torn" setting. Williams went on to identify five key features central to the melodramatic mode. Let's consider "The Last Beat of My Heart" within this framework. First, Williams suggests that "Melodrama begins, and wants to end in a space of innocence."[11] Check. This innocence—and the purity with which it is conveyed—is embodied in Sioux's vocality.

Elevated and refined, on "The Last Beat of My Heart" Sioux's dialect is as close to perfection a vocal performance gets as she delivers the track in her best "Queen's English" with regal command. Every single word of the song is delicately framed with a reverb so light and ghostly, it's as though we are hearing her sing this from another—almost mythological—world entirely, not unlike Galadriel from *The Lord of the Rings*.[12] This voice is reserved only for "The Last Beat of My Heart": authoritative, pronounced, and *pure* Sioux's vocal demands our special attention. In saying that, her voice retains a compelling fragility with subtle trills and vibrato convincing us that these are indeed words of someone experiencing a dying love, both literally and metaphorically. Budgie's introductory timpani and McCarrick's gradually approaching accordion construct a grand entrance, an appropriately vast stage upon which this epic love story plays out. The hold— the *spell*—this introduction casts on us listeners is prolonged by Severin's synth with lengthy, hypnotic string-like chords, as his intention was to "express the fear of separation."[13] The lead protagonist's purity is established almost immediately; this is a love song and the image of a rose is presented early in the first verse. And, of course, this innocence continues throughout the track until the end. Williams's second feature of melodrama is that it "focuses on victim-heroes and the recognition of their virtue."[14] Once again this is established early on in the track, since we are dealing with heroes whose love has traversed a war, yet the survival of this love is uncertain. The timeframe is, however, unclear. The love is first described as a memory yet the underscoring of the line beginning "we" with an ethereal, double-tracked echo

(0.38) denotes the presence of the lover. This double-tracked line reinforces the protagonists' virtue and continues as the synth breaks from its lengthy sustained chords into a staccato triplet rhythm building momentum (0.58), pre-empting the vocal rhythm. At this point, the lovers are apart. Lines delivered in triplet onomatopoeia, matching the synth and sailing as if over waves, underscore the vast distance between the lovers and implies their separation by sea:

Sol—i—tude
Sails—in—a
Wave—of—for
Give—ness—on

However, Siouxsie and the Banshees' trademark ambiguity disrupts our protagonists' virtues: yes, we have words like "forgiveness" and "angels" evoking purity and holiness, but prior to this we hear references to a thorn and shame, both representative of sin. The "Bridge of Sighs" (0.52) too is a reference to the seventeenth-century enclosed bridge in Venice, passing over the Rio de Palazzo and connecting the New Prison with Doge's Palace, which, inspired by Roxy Music's "Song for Europe," Severin included to portray "a sense of decaying grandeur."[15] This historical gaze—this time analogized to crime, punishment, and confinement in seventeenth-century Italy—is immediately followed up with the word "solitude"; at least one of these lovers is imprisoned, albeit metaphorically. This sense of longing in isolation is augmented with a further distortion of time, for at 0.59— the only point in the song—the meter diverts to 5/4 for a single bar before reverting back to 4/4 as if extending and emphasizing this isolation.

Williams's third feature of the melodramatic mode pertains to realism as she states, "Melodrama appears modern by borrowing from realism, but realism serves the melodramatic passion and action."[16] With such a strong historical and mythological aesthetic, few elements of "The Last Beat of My Heart" could be construed as realism. Yet a clear, albeit swift, reference occurs during the second verse. Before we look at that, there are other, deeply filmic aspects inherent to verse two worth exploring. I argue that the second verse of "The Last Beat of My Heart" is *Peepshow*'s most profound moment. In epic film, Tom Brown recognized "the hilltop or similar vantage point appears particularly suited to the inscription of the 'big history' to come and the character's recognition of his/ her place in it."[17] A classic example of this landscape staging lies in Victor Fleming's epic *Gone with the Wind* (1939) at the key turning point in the film. Scarlett is horrified to arrive back at Tara to see it war torn, her father incompetent, and her mother dead. She walks out into the ravaged, deracinated land, raises her fist and defiantly says in an iconic scene "As God is my witness, I'll never be hungry again."[18] Here, the *reality* of Scarlett's situation and the enormity of the task she faces in rebuilding Tara underlines *Gone with the Wind*'s significant melodramatic turning point. At a key moment in "The Last Beat of My Heart," Sioux is similarly staged as she overstates her situ as "here and now" while dramatically positioning herself against a sunset vista backdrop. (Incidentally, yet another reference to the technical aspects of film is made here with reference to "shadow play.")

This filmic stage occurs in the middle of the song (2.02) and is wholly in line with Sioux's intention that the song should not be a "small statement."[19] But this is only the beginning. The overstated "here and now" is the point of realism in the track; this is not history, memory, reminiscence, imaginary, or nostalgia, neither are we anywhere in the future. This important line underscores *Peepshow*'s most melodramatic moment, as Brown suggested, "Melodrama and melodramatic performance are also often characterized by an emotionally charged gaze into space."[20] In this instance, we have a gaze followed by a lengthy cry. Such a grand pretext befits the lines to follow—and I am certain that even the most hardcore Siouxsie and the Banshees fans would not disagree when I say these are quite possibly the band's most profound:

> And the naked bone of an echo says,
> "Don't walk away"

In his groundbreaking work on Hollywood melodrama, Elsaesser stated, "Pathos results from non-communication or silence made eloquent."[21] The construction of such affecting, such heart-wrenching pathos in a vocal delivery so impeccable manifests at 2.34. Sioux performs "The Last Beat of My Heart" from first-person perspective, yet the haunting, ghostly echo of long lost love is briefly personified in its reverberant, ethereal response to her lead protagonist that—just for one line—becomes the narrator: this echo is silence made eloquent. We hear this very construction of a voice from beyond in Joe Meek's production on John Leyton's hit "Johnny Remember Me" (1961); one of Sioux's favorite singles, she described hearing it as "that first delicious feeling of subversion."[22] On "The Last Beat of My Heart" we hear less a reference to the comical but ultimately implausible sound of a voice from the grave, but in borrowing Meek's production aesthetic (as opposed to Leyton's delivery), and performing the lines so sincerely, we hear a more sophisticated and convincing construction of a ghost. At this critical point, we hear *Peepshow*—we hear Siouxsie and the Banshees—at the very pinnacle of epic. And it's not over yet.

Williams's fourth aspect of melodrama "involves a dialectic of pathos and action—a give and take of 'too late' and 'in the nick of time.'"[23] This temporal tension forms the lynchpin to "The Last Beat of My Heart"—and is embodied in its title. Throughout, we hear multiple suggestions that these lovers are just a moment from reuniting in a torturous play on this "so near and yet so far" dynamic. This dialectic of pathos and action is reinforced lyrically, particularly at the end of the track, with "a step away" (2.48) and "last fleeting beat" (3.37). Musically, however, it is Klein's guitar that perfectly interprets this dynamic. His ebow-esque swells mirror the lovers near/afar proximity, the fleeting nature of presence and absence. Consider this mechanism at its most prominent, in the bridge between 0.53 and 0.59. Also, during verse two: the guitar is silent until 2.31, swelling until confrontationally foregrounded before quickly disappearing by 2.35. This same technique occurs between 2.40 and 2.42.

Finally, Williams suggests that melodrama "presents characters who embody primary psychic roles organized in Manichaean conflicts between good and evil."[24] Ultimately, "The Last Beat of My Heart" is a classic tale of love enduring, if not conquering, all. Particularly war. This dualistic structure of love and war is integral to the war epic, exploited to maximum effect in films such as *Casablanca* (1942). Sioux mentioned this film as inspiring *Kaleidoscope*'s "Desert Kisses" (1980),[25] but there is a stronger connection to the melodramatic mode in "The Last Beat of My Heart." Michael Curtiz's World War II epic melodrama situates lead protagonists Rick and Ilsa in the Moroccan city, where US expatriate Rick owns a nightclub and Ilsa, along with her husband Victor, are stranded and trying to return to America. That Rick and Ilsa were former lovers sets up a classic love triangle; the tension between Rick and Ilsa is underscored by a combination of Herman Hupfield's "As Time Goes By" with the French national anthem "La Marseillaise." This combination, perfectly meshed by composer Max Steiner, effortlessly shifts the filmic mood to and fro between the long lost love and the realities of war. As repetitive as Steiner's score is, its constant mechanism steadies the narrative's emotional unpredictability, as Paul Allen Anderson suggests,

> Steiner's deeply repetitive orchestral music works especially hard to slow things down, to make things matter. His score returns . . . to its pseudo-Wagnerian leitmotifs of regret . . . and love, in order to charge the . . . action with the force of . . . conviction.[26]

A significant parallel can be drawn between the musical mechanism in "The Last Beat of My Heart" and that in Steiner's *Casablanca* score. Of all *Peepshow*'s tracks, "The Last Beat of My Heart" is the least musically complex; such an affecting, foregrounded vocal would not work against a busy musical backdrop. To that end, Budgie's timpani rhythm—

undoubtedly a heartbeat metaphor—and Severin's synth chords are both rhythmically and dynamically repetitive, laying a constant, reliable foundation. As previously mentioned, Klein's guitar analogizes the push and pull of presence and absence, but it is McCarrick's accordion that symbolizes the lovers' hope, for unification and for peace. In *Casablanca*, Rick and Ilsa's affair played out in Paris. The memory montage featuring the Champs-Élysées, as well as the lovers' most intimate dancehall and hotel moments, are some of the film's most memorable. It is this very nostalgia for the world's most romantic city that is evoked by McCarrick's accordion in "The Last Beat of My Heart." As Phil Powrie pointed out, the accordion signifies "a precise location—Paris . . . romance with a whiff of the exotic . . . which turns the banal and the everyday into the sophisticated and the exceptional."[27]

In joining Severin's synth rhythm with a prominent triplet harmony, McCarrick's accordion leads the coda (3.47) in a swirling waltz poised above the timpani's constant 4/4. Ghostly voices, like those used to double-track earlier lines, constructed almost entirely from reverb channels fade in and out of this sentimental, yet steady and controlled finale lasting almost a minute. The ways in which these melodic lines ebb and flow are almost identical to Steiner's score, as described by Paul Allen Anderson, in *Casablanca*

> the circulating flow of melodies and leitmotifs acts to fill up a powerful reservoir of constancy, an invisible reservoir into which past romantic and political certainties can be stored and from which they can be accessed as present certainties.[28]

There is a sense of vast spectacle in "The Last Beat of My Heart" that the band never achieved before or since. And to that point, we can draw a further parallel to Fleming's *Gone with the Wind*. Brown called the film a "monument"[29] in Hollywood cinema, yet simultaneously a "monumental anomaly,"[30] due to its never-to-be-repeated *epicness* of character, length, location, costume, and overall *mise en scène*. We can, of course, say the same about "The Last Beat of My Heart." It's a one-off. A stand out single in Siouxsie and the Banshees' career, yet an anomaly—indicative of nothing else in their repertoire.

"Rhapsody"

Despite *Peepshow*'s ambiguous, surrealist aesthetic, overall the album retains a sense of playful optimism missing from most of the band's previous studio albums. That is, until "Rhapsody"—*Peepshow*'s epic, albeit bleak, finale. Vivian Sobchack recognized how the Hollywood epic "defines History as occurring to music—pervasive symphonic music underscoring every moment by overscoring it."[31] "Rhapsody" draws on this genre aesthetic with its juxtaposing of barren minimalism and densely textured orchestration, the latter overscoring a stark, dystopian historical narrative.

In 1988, Sioux described "Rhapsody" as written about

[Dmitri] Shostakovich, a really sad man who was victimised, ridiculed and then broken by the Stalin regime. I love his music, really powerful. The song's about wishing you could have been a consolation to him.[32]

This is a revealing perspective since Sioux appears so personally attached to the song, yet Severin—and *not* Sioux—is credited with writing it. Dmitri Shostakovich (1906–1975) is one of the most celebrated and revered composers in both Russian and wider classical music history. Musicological studies on the works of Shostakovich, an icon of modernism, are plentiful, yet most attempt to unravel the political and moral subtexts present in his music and many present a well-worn theory that Shostakovich's public face was one of compliant communist yet behind this façade was a dissident and Shostakovich communicated this, his true political stance, through his symphonies. Four years after his death in 1975, Russian musicologist Solomon Volkov published *Testimony* (1979),[33] a controversial work that reinforced this theory and claimed to be the memoirs of the famous composer, the result of multiple interviews in the years leading up to his death. During the early 1970s, Volkov claimed Shostakovich

> no longer consoled himself with the thought that music could express everything and did not require verbal commentary. His works now spoke with mounting power of only one thing: impending death.[34]

In her book *Shostakovich: A Life Remembered*, Elizabeth Wilkinson warns against the "dramatic allure"[35] of Volkov's—and other scholars—"extreme representation"[36] of Shostakovich and encourages a more balanced view of his contribution to music. With its stark soundscape staging an ominous sense of foreboding, "Rhapsody" does, however, draw from the Volkovian perspective,[37] as Sioux suggested,

[Shostakovich] had a very hard life. A lot of his contemporaries, who were victims of the Stalin era, all ended up being martyrs. . . . But Shostakovich did the unforgivable and made slight compromises so that he could continue working. It was so sad. They criticised his work viciously and then, when people came back round to praising it, it wasn't enough. "Rhapsody" . . . really should have been dedicated to him.[38]

Throughout their career, Siouxsie and the Banshees regularly cited Shostakovich's most revered compositions and the earliest such reference occurred in 1980—one year after Volkov's *Testimony*. In *Modern Drummer*, Budgie stated Symphony No. 5 in D Minor (Op. 47, 1937) was his first go-to piece for inspiration.[39] This symphony signified a turning point in Shostakovich's career, since it followed state denunciation of his opera, *Lady Macbeth of the Mtsensk District* (Op. 29, 1934) and his withdrawal of Symphony No. 4 in C Minor (Op. 43, 1936) due to strong themes of tragedy that, had the symphony been performed, ". . . would have provoked horrible controversy."[40] In a dangerous political position, Shostakovich wrote No. 5, a triumphant, evocative symphony in four movements against a backdrop of the

great purges and "show trials," where Stalin's political enemies were forced into abject confessions and humiliation prior to their liquidation. Stalin imposed the Terror so as to transform all institutions—the Party, heavy industry and the armed forces—into obedient tools.[41]

Critically, in a newspaper article a few days before the premiere, a journalist pitched Symphony No. 5 as "A Soviet

Artist's Creative Response to Just Criticism." Shostakovich allowed this description "to remain in programmes . . . which could be interpreted as an admission of his errors and gesture of repentance."[42] In *Shostakovich Against Stalin: The War Symphonies*, composer Vladimir Rubin went further and stated of the fifth symphony,

> It was during a very difficult time. A time of terror in our country. Many people close to Shostakovich were swept away by this bloody meat grinder. This symphony (5th) was crucial for his destiny because his very life was on the brink of extinction.[43]

By 1949, Shostakovich was denounced once again for perceived formalism and dismissed from the Leningrad Conservatory where he worked. Around this time, Shostakovich grew to rely on film music scoring for an income, composing for state propaganda films that portrayed Stalin in an exaggerated, heroic light. One of these films, *The Fall of Berlin* (1950) features a particularly rousing score by Shostakovich, what John Riley noted as being "one of the most fascinating documents of this time"[44] and that "the saturation level of propaganda—and how Shostakovich responds to it—is one of the very things that makes [*The Fall of Berlin* and other films] interesting."[45] Shostakovich's film music scores are the most understudied in his repertoire—I'll return to this a bit later on.

The specificity of Sioux's consolation of Shostakovich, however, goes further than Tom Brown's "excess of detail" in the historical spectacle. Sioux is placed in this history as a protagonist that, presumably with Shostakovich, continues with fading optimism, hanging on to their dreams against a backdrop of brutality, of genocide. This opportunity—and ability—to insert oneself as a character in a historical narrative they were never originally part of is the very essence of epic film genre, as Sobchack suggested,

> The importance of the [historical epic] genre is not that it narrates and dramatizes historical events accurately according to the detailed stories of academic historians but rather that it opens a temporal field that creates the general possibility for recognizing oneself as a historical subject of a particular kind.[46]

In an extensive work on the aesthetics of epic in film, Constantine Santas analyzed the classic epic form as featuring seven key constituents:

a. length

b. unified action

c. multiple plots

d. hero

e. pity and fear

f. happy resolutions, and

g. spectacle.[47]

Let's consider how "Rhapsody" works within this framework. At more than six minutes in length, "Rhapsody" is not structured like a typical popular song. Neither does it resemble a rhapsody since, structurally, such compositions feature irregular form and suggest improvisation. The form in

"Rhapsody" is closer to a symphony in two movements; one slow (*adagio*—0–1.14) into a quick fast (*allegro*—1.14–6.24) and as such, closes the album exactly as it begins: with a track bearing more resemblance to art music than popular. As a songwriter, this was always Severin's intention, "I loved the crossover of fine art into music, it really took it somewhere else."[48] The initial, lengthy minimalist staging in "Rhapsody" is notable for its ominousness. Creeping in with the same approach as "The Last Beat of My Heart," this time a call-and-answer synth motif responds to each line of the first verse. Klein's subtle, yet heavily delayed pick sweeps (0.32; 0.36; 0.40; and ongoing) cut through lengthy synthesized string chords as the pick repeats fall away to nothing, emphasizing the desolate, post-genocidal world in which these protagonists are staged. Santas's components of epic also recognize unified action, which does not "attempt to treat an entire historical period that lasts several decades," but instead focuses on dramatizing a specific point in time. According to Santas,[49] unified action could be present in plot coherence, such as in William Wyler's *Ben Hur* (1959) or in unity of character, such as in David Lean's *Lawrence of Arabia* (1962). "Rhapsody" traces the plight of two characters— presumably Sioux and Shostakovich—in existential crisis, considering their past, "a time of rapture," and hopeless future with nothing but their dreams to hold on to. Verse one presents these characters as unified (understood by the use of "our") and desperate, attempting to draw upon the last trace of their fast-fading hope.

During verse one, Sioux's exhausted protagonist labors her only place of sanctuary: a refuge she finds in a choral lament, serenaded by a choir. She recalls this music from deep within her heart, which in turn is buried in her sadness. Here, there is a critical link between the choral lament faintly recalled by Sioux's protagonist in the midst of devastation, and Shostakovich's most memorable choral lamentation, part of his score to Grigori Kosintsev's Soviet adaptation of *King Lear* (1971). The score to Kosintsev's take on the Shakespeare play was one of Shostakovich's final works and featured fanfares, a blend of incidental music and key musical sections to underscore the narrative. As described by Kosintsev, at the time Shostakovich was ill and "how much worse [he] looks. He limps and can no longer play his music. He has been ill for a long time. His hand has shriveled up, his bones brittle."[50] Both director and composer agreed on a theme of "grief and misfortune"[51] for *King Lear*'s score; this intense emotive expression resembling some of Shostakovich's finest symphonies. As Olga Dombrovskai suggested "In the composition of the Lamentation, this virtually final film composition by Shostakovich, the differences between film music and instrumental, non-programmatic music have disappeared."[52] In Shostakovich's score, Op. 137,[53] the choral lament is positioned as a pause between two movements depicting a heavy storm. In "Rhapsody," the first verse reprise at 4.11 and could be read in the same way; a sudden dynamic drop sandwiched between two highly percussive, densely textured symphonic sections and featuring the identical lyrics recalling the choral lament. There is another layer here too, since the song's two minute-long, densely textured segments (3.14–4.11 and 4.36–5.34) too resemble a storm; the swirling orchestration is suddenly whipped up from nowhere before circling around the voice like a tornado. I'll return to these sections later on.

In verse two we hear Siouxsie and the Banshees evoke violence without explicitly referencing it. Sioux's reference to the band as "blood splashed on a daisy in the sunshine"[54] returns in "Rhapsody," as lines such as "In the blood of the twinkling sky" evoke a horrifying dystopia. Yet in the midst of this nightmare, there is hope: the bell, the twinkling, the choir, the gleaming all point to the possibility of escape.

Returning to Santos's epic constructs, multiple plots and the presence of the hero are both integral to the diegesis of "Rhapsody." We have the protagonists' despair and hope, their looking to the past and future, their dreams and their resignation as Stalin wages war against his own people. In "Rhapsody," the two protagonists are undoubtedly heroic and the band does a fine job of creating juxtaposing sonic stages to match their plight, oscillating between safety and peril throughout. At 1.14, their hope is interrupted with a major reality check. Budgie's urgent eighth-note hi-hat and snare rim shot progression is reinforced by Klein's dampened arpeggios; high paced and tense, this taut combination places our protagonists in immediate danger. Budgie and Klein maintain the tension throughout, with Klein's occasionally foregrounded rung-through arpeggios (1.26) in the midst of tight, dampened picks analogizes the character's fear—another of Santos's epic aesthetics—as it builds and recedes. Of course, in order for the protagonists to assume a heroic role there must be a villain, an enemy. Here, another Siouxsie and the Banshees trademark, the nursery rhyme allusion, is used to stage this villain. This time the "crooked man" (1.42) is used as an analogy for Stalin, yet the poem originated in mid-nineteenth-century England from the Stuart history of King Charles I.[55] The "stile" is understood to represent the division between England and Scotland, and the "house" the eventual unification of the two countries:

> There was a crooked man and he walked a crooked mile
> He found a crooked sixpence upon a crooked stile
> He bought a crooked cat, which caught a crooked mouse
> And they all lived together in a little crooked house.[56]

Despite its English origin, the position of this nursery rhyme allusion in the Soviet-based "Rhapsody" works due to the common theme of war. And after witnessing their loved ones die, our heroic pair turn their attention to each other and face their own mortality. This switch of focus is defined by a synth motif (1.57–2.03), a clear demarcation between what the protagonists have witnessed and the realization of their own impending fate. This pivotal moment in the song epitomizes the notion of epic and in holding this critical point for the duration of a verse (2.03–2.27), the band underscore its significance. Rudolf Arnheim recognized this technique of prolonging key moments as inherent to epic film form, as he stated "Externally, a man's entanglement with time appears as dynamic or dramatic because the passing of time suggests a progression; but basically it is static and epic."[57]

What lends "Rhapsody" its sense of extravagance is the musical juxtaposition of minimalism and symphony. Until 2.27 the song is carried by Sioux's voice and musically, aside from rhythmic changes, the track is relatively sparse. But this musical retention mechanism only serves to elevate the song texturally and dynamically later on. A dramatic build is created with a foregrounded acoustic guitar, emphasizing "I" (2.27) and "seen" (2.29), "I" (2.33) and "felt" (2.35), and "Rhapsody" (2.39, 2.45). This transition allows us listeners time to refocus on the protagonists and their feelings after hearing their harrowing witness to genocide. At this point, the instrumentation begins to swell; Severin's bass instigates this dramatic rise by shifting from a whole note/eighth-note pattern into repetitive eighth-notes (2.51), increasing in urgency and filling out the lower register with an ominous rumble. Severin's bass and the synthesized strings are brought level with the acoustic guitar and by 3.02 Budgie's urgent percussive rolls build simultaneous to the strings underscoring the word "Rhapsody" (3.02, 3.09), his crashing cymbals and chimes evoking the onset of a storm.

Later on in the track, the symphonic sections (3.14–4.11 and 4.36–5.34) envelop the quieter verse one reprise and parallels between this structure and that of Shostakovich's *King Lear* have already been drawn. These heavily orchestrated sections may also be read as evoking *Peepshow*'s pre-production, storm-ravaged *mise en scène* of Ardingly. The sheer ferocity and might with which these sections are performed by all band members suggests the very "excess of action" that Brown suggested is a key constituent of epic,[58] and more specifically, of *spectacle*. Let's consider these sections in more detail, because not only do they resemble a storm but, on an orchestration level, they can be read as indicating the presence of military: our protagonists now narrate from the midst of the war action.

From 3.14, Budgie's crash cymbals accentuate off beats, and then change to a staccato four-note repeat at 3.23 in a "stabbing" motion. At 3.28 this pattern is repeated and joined by the strings, which reinforces this sense of attack of repetitive striking. The four-note cymbal repeat is played again at 3.34. During this section Sioux's voice, until now the most prominent instrument in the mix, is gradually enveloped by the rising intensity of percussion, bass, guitar, and strings. As she realizes she has seen and felt all she wants to (3.14–3.25), and in turning to her hero to remind him they will always have their dreams (3.26–3.36), we become aware of what our heroes know: they are going to die. Here, we have yet another of Siouxsie and the Banshees' trademark paracinematic twists. For if "Rhapsody" was drawn from conservative, Hollywood epic it would play out precisely as Santos recognized in epic form: everyone would live happily ever after. But unlike "The Last Beat of My Heart," "Rhapsody" is not drawn from Hollywood tradition, but an earlier one: the Soviet proto-epics of Sergei Eisenstein.

In the middle of World War I, Russia's ruling Tsarist autocracy was destroyed in two revolutions signifying the beginning of the rise of the Soviet Union. Out of this era grew Russia's national cinema, which, as Brian Robb suggested, developed in isolation in a similar way to Germany's film industry. Russian cinema did, however, have a "clear ideological purpose, a medium to be used to 'educate' and 'enlighten' the proletariat population."[59] Vladimir Lenin, and Joseph Stalin later on, used cinema as an effective means of disseminating propaganda and as such, cinema—as well as scores, soundtracks, and other art forms—were almost entirely under state control. Severin's approach to capturing a historical moment in "Rhapsody" resembles Eisenstein's approach to his most significant cinematic work *The Battleship Potemkin* (1925). Based on the 1905 revolution, this iconic propaganda film follows the crew of a ship, Potemkin, as they stage a mutiny against their officers. The film is particularly notable for Eisenstein's use of montage in the "Odessa Steps" sequence, since canonized as one of the most influential film sequences in cinematic history. However, as Richard Taylor pointed out, while the mutiny was based on true events, the military confrontation depicted in the Odessa Steps sequence was dramatized as

> a classic example of poetic license: a filmic creation of a historical event that in itself never happened but that encapsulates in microcosm the macrocosmic drama of a more general historical process.[60]

This brutal montage, which depicts the assassination of a mother, the bloodied face of a school headmistress, and a baby in a pram falling down the steps among other horrific imagery, is set against an equally affecting score by Edward Meisel. As Taylor went on to say,

> These characters represent a Vorschlag—to use Eisenstein's own term—of the storm that is about to break, a storm whose imminence was indicated by the very opening sequences of the film.[61]

Meisel's dynamic score accentuates the mood of the ship's crew as it ebbs and flows between calm and frenetic, simultaneous to the movement of the ship and the onset of a storm. For example, in Part 1: The Men and the Maggots, Meisel's bombastic orchestral phrases featuring prominent cymbals and percussion accompany the doctor's exit from the ship; the music then softening to a bass-heavy string section with staccato pizzicato as the crew prepare a meal. There are significant similarities between Meisel's scoring of the Odessa Steps sequence and the second of two symphonic sections in "Rhapsody" (4.36–5.34). Out of the word *refuge*, we hear Sioux's ascending glissando curl up among the onset of heavy strings and percussion. Budgie once again punctuates this symphony, this time with an eighth-note crash cymbal repeat (4.39) following up with an even punchier sixteenth-note staccato (4.44) in unison with the strings—this time, with an added timpani-like drum, which continues until 4.53. This foregrounding of percussion and strings is identical to Meisel's scoring of the militaristic Odessa Steps scenes in *The Battleship Potemkin*. Consider Tom Armstrong's description of the score at this point:

> Composer Meisel parallels the implacable descent of the Tsarist troops with a relentless, percussive pounding overlaid with grotesque parodies of military brass tattoos and sinewy, chromatic phrases in the strings.[62]

The cacophony of strings and percussion is held to a crescendo, with further striking snare and string motifs on eighth-notes (4.50), then breaking into quarter-notes (4.56) before Sioux reaches her highest vocal pitch on *Peepshow*. The song reaches its peak (5.02–5.09) with the return of the timpani underscoring the percussion and string stabs, as Sioux's vocality turns to a soprano-like cry, desperate and overwhelmed as the instrumentation encircles her. Our protagonist's final attempt at breaking through the relentless orchestration occurs at 5.22 with a repetitive high-pitched holler, joined by Klein's electric guitar for a quarter-note phrase at 5.25. This extraordinary reconstruction of military action again resembles Meisel's score, as Armstrong suggested his

> music, taking its cue from the rhythm of the troops' marching feet, focuses relentlessly on the brutality of the authorities, avoiding any identification with the fate of individuals.[63]

During the extended coda, we hear the music and voice work in opposition as opposed to in unison. The percussion, which signified the protagonists' emotions earlier in the track, is now working against them. In *Peepshow*'s press release, Severin stated "Rhapsody" was "more about the human spirit than any particular political situation."[64] This spirit is captured in the coda; Sioux's voice recedes as echoes and delays reverberate the dying words of a heroine at the conclusion of this monumental war epic.

"Rhapsody" is *Peepshow*'s most emotive track, building on the melodrama in "The Last Beat of My Heart" with an evocative portrayal of destruction, danger, and depression. Its modernist structure and densely textured form juxtapose the sparse radiophonics of *Peepshow*'s opener, closing the record with a highly orchestrated historical gaze into the horrors of genocide.

* * *

Siouxsie and the Banshees chose to conclude *Peepshow* with a declaration of their love for Shostakovich and the wider Soviet classicist canon. This finale—and *Peepshow* as a whole—cemented the band as lone pioneers of a pop/rock middlebrow in an otherwise utilitarian commercial music landscape; few achieve at this nexus of high and low culture, particularly from the popular music side. The Velvet Underground and Nico traversed the middlebrow in the context of 1960s counterculture; Bowie did so against a kaleidoscopic glam. Yet Siouxsie and the Banshees achieved this same feat in 1988—a point in their career when they were peerless, when popular music ate itself via samplers, SSL recall, and multi-remix form, during factory-production trio Stock, Aitken, and Waterman's peak, the onset of genuinely new popular music forms including hip hop and house. Remarkable then, that this unique record was the band's then-most successful during the reinvented popular music landscape of the late 1980s. Yet in its slow-burn influence on other musicians, *Peepshow*'s endurance lingers on; this is not the *definitive* Banshees record, neither a "classic" Banshees record—that title probably belongs to *Juju* or *Join Hands*—but *Peepshow* is undoubtedly the band's most realized and accomplished record. Because *Peepshow* represents everything Siouxsie and the Banshees were artistically, musically, and conceptually, it sounds like the record they were always trying to make, the record they were always working toward. Like classical music, which "cherishes this idea of transcending the time and place in which a work was written,"[65] *Peepshow* attempted exactly the same thing. And succeeded.

This book has focused on reading *Peepshow* through a filmic lens and in doing so cites more than one hundred films, the majority of which are known influences on the band. We might then consider *Peepshow* as a soundtrack to all the films Siouxsie and the Banshees ever saw. Or perhaps it was the soundtrack to the greatest film they never made. Either way, as Sioux reflected, "We were making soundtracks for the films in our heads."[66]

Acknowledgments

This book was completed with the support of two research fellowships. For the first, a Case Western Reserve University/ Rock and Roll Hall of Fame Library and Archives fellowship, I extend my deepest gratitude to Dr. Daniel Goldmark, Andy Leach, and Jennie Thomas. I am most thankful to Professor Will Christie, Head of the Humanities Research Centre (HRC) at the Australian National University, for awarding me with an internal research fellowship in Semester 2, 2016. This book would not have been as detailed nor realized without that time in the HRC. With thanks to colleagues in the IASPM, EMP Museum (MoPop), EuroMAC, and SurreyMAC fora for their insightful and helpful feedback following conference presentations of the research contained in this book. I am eternally grateful to Peter Routley for keeping such a comprehensive chronological record of Siouxsie and the Banshees' press coverage over the course of their career on *thebansheesandothercreatures.co.uk* and in his fantastic press collection, *Songs: From the Edge of the World*. My sincerest thanks to Costas Christodopoulos for his very generous and diligent assistance over many months in scanning hard-to-find magazine articles. Some of the interview citations present in this book would not have been so accurate without Costas's assistance. Also, many thanks to Franck Carlier for translating European articles to ensure I could reference accurately. I would also like to thank Ronnie Randall for providing me with a scan of his article in *Offbeat* magazine, which is not held in national libraries. With thanks to the staff in the Humanities Reading Room at the British Library and Chifley Library at the Australian National University. With thanks to former 33 1/3 editor Ally Jane Grossan for choosing this proposal from more than six hundred others in 2015. I am still blown away that you chose this book for the series. I am most grateful to 33 1/3 editor Leah Babb-Rosenfeld for her support and guidance, and to Michelle Chen, for her most helpful and detailed editing and suggestions as I completed the manuscript. Thanks always to my family and friends for their love and patience. And finally, thank you to Siouxsie, Severin, Budgie, Martin, Jon, and Mike for making such an extraordinary record.

With love
Sam
February 2018

Films Cited

Amiel, Jon. *The Singing Detective*. UK: BBC, 1986.

Brooks, Mel. *Blazing Saddles*. 92 minutes. United States: Warner Bros., 1974.

Buñuel, Luis. *Un Chien Andalou*. 17 minutes. France: Les Grandes Films Classiques, 1929.

Buñuel, Luis. *L'Age D'or*. 63 minutes. France: Corinth Films, 1930.

Capra, Frank. *It's a Wonderful Life*. 130 minutes. United States: RKO Radio Pictures, 1946.

Chaplin, Charles. *The Circus*. 70 minutes. United States: United Artists, 1928.

Chiaureli, Mikheil. *The Fall of Berlin*. 167 minutes. Soviet Union: Aminko, 1950.

Clayton, Jack. *Something Wicked This Way Comes*. 95 minutes. United States: Buena Vista Distribution, 1983.

Cline, Edward F. and Keaton, Buster. *The Scarecrow*. 19 minutes. United States: Metro Pictures, 1920.

Coppola, Francis Ford. *The Outsiders*. 110 minutes. United States: Warner Bros., 1983.

Coppola, Francis Ford. *Rumble Fish*. 94 minutes. United States: Universal Pictures, 1983.

Corman, Roger. *House of Usher*. 79 minutes. United States: American International Pictures, 1960.

Corman, Roger. *The Pit and the Pendulum*. 85 minutes. United States: American International Pictures, 1961.

Corman, Roger. *The Masque of the Red Death*. 90 minutes. United States: American International Pictures, 1964.

Craven, Wes. *A Nightmare on Elm Street*. 91 minutes. United States: New Line Cinema, 1984.

Curtiz, Michael. *Casablanca*. 102 minutes. United States: Warner Bros., 1942.

Dickson, William K. L. and William Heise. *Sioux Ghost Dance*. 1 minute. United States: Edison Manufacturing Company, 1894.

Dickson, William K. L. and William Heise. *Buffalo Dance*. 1 minute. United States: Edison Manufacturing Company, 1894.

Donen, Stanley. *Kiss Them for Me*. 105 minutes. United States: 20th Century Fox, 1957.

Donner, Richard. *The Omen*. 111 minutes. United States, United Kingdom: 20th Century Fox, 1976.

Eastwood, Clint. *Pale Rider*. 116 minutes. United States: Warner Bros., 1985.

Edison Manufacturing Company. *Railroad Smashup*. 37 seconds. Boston, MA, United States: Edison Manufacturing Company, 1904.

Eisenstein, Sergei. *The Battleship Potemkin*. 75 minutes. Soviet Union: Goskino, 1925.

Enright, Ray. *Going Places*. 84 minutes. United States: Warner Bros., 1938.

Fellini, Federico. *Casanova*. 155 minutes. Italy: Universal Studios, 1976.

Ferguson, Norm et al. *Fantasia*. 125 minutes. United States: Walt Disney Productions, 1940.

Fleming, Victor. *The Wizard of Oz*. 101 minutes: Metro-Goldwyn-Mayer, 1939.

Fleming, Victor. *Gone with the Wind*. 224 minutes. United States: Loew's Inc, 1939.

Forbes, Bryan. *The Stepford Wives*. 115 minutes. United States: Columbia Pictures, 1975.

Fosse, Bob. *Cabaret*. 124 minutes. United States: Allied Artists, 1972.

Friedkin, William. *The Exorcist*. 121 minutes. United States: Warner Bros., 1973.

Garnett, Tay. *The Postman Always Rings Twice*. 113 minutes. United States: Metro-Goldwyn-Mayer, 1946.

Hanley, Francis. *Bernard Herrmann*. In *Howard Goodall's 20th Century Greats*. UK: Tiger Aspect Productions, 2004.

Hardy, Robin. *The Wicker Man*. 87 minutes. UK: British Lion Films, 1973.

Haskin, Byron. "Demon with a Glass Hand." In *The Outer Limits*, edited by Leslie Stevens, 51 minutes. United States: ABC, 1964.

Heerman, Victor. *Animal Crackers*. 96 minutes. United States: Paramount Pictures, 1930.

Heise, William. *Parade of Buffalo Bill's Wild West Show, No. 1* (1 minute) *and No. 2*. (2 minutes) United States: Edison Manufacturing Company, 1898.

Hessler, Gordon. *Cry of the Banshee*. 87 minutes. UK: American International Pictures, 1970.

Hitchcock, Alfred. *Spellbound*. 111 minutes. United States: United Artists, 1945.

Hitchcock, Alfred. *Strangers on a Train*. 101 minutes. United States: Warner Bros., 1951.

Hitchcock, Alfred. *Rear Window*. 112 minutes. United States: Paramount Pictures, 1954.

Hitchcock, Alfred. *Vertigo*. 128 minutes. United States: Paramount Pictures, 1958.

Hitchcock, Alfred. *Psycho*. 109 minutes. United States: Paramount Pictures, 1960.

Hooper, Tobe. *The Fun House*. 96 minutes. United States: Universal Pictures, 1981.

Hooper, Tobe. *Poltergeist*. 114 minutes. United States: MGM/UA Entertainment Co., 1982.

Hunt, Peter R. *Gold*. 120 minutes. UK/Republic of South Africa: Allied Artists, 1974.

Huston, John. *The Treasure of the Sierra Madre*. 126 minutes. United States: Warner Bros., 1948.

King, Henry. *Carousel*. 128 minutes. United States: 20th Century Fox, 1956.

Kozintsev, Grigori. *King Lear*. 130 minutes. Soviet Union: Lenfilm, 1971.

Kubrick, Stanley. *The Shining*. 119 minutes. United States: Warner Bros., 1980.

Lang, Fritz. *Metropolis*. 153 minutes (original) 148 minutes (restoration). Weimar Republic: UFA, 1927.

Lang, Fritz. *M*. 111 minutes. Weimar Republic: Vereinigite Star-Film GmbH, 1931.

Lang, Walter. *The King and I*. 133 minutes. United States: 20th Century Fox, 1956.

Lean, David. *Lawrence of Arabia*. 222 minutes. United States: Columbia Pictures, 1962.

Leone, Sergio. *The Good, the Bad and the Ugly*. 177 minutes. United States: United Artists, 1966.

Leone, Sergio. *Once Upon a Time in the West*. 165 minutes. United States: Paramount Pictures, 1968.

Logan, Joshua. *South Pacific*. 171 minutes. United States: 20th Century Fox, 1958.

Lumière, Auguste, and Louis Lumière. *L'arrivée D'un Train En Gare De La Ciotat*. 50 seconds. Paris, France: Société Lumière, 1896.

Lynch, David. *Eraserhead*. 88 minutes. United States: Libra Films International, 1977.

Lynch, David. *Blue Velvet*. 120 minutes. United States: De Laurentiis Entertainment Group, 1986.

Mankiewicz, Joseph L. *Cleopatra*. 248 minutes. United States: 20th Century Fox, 1963.

Marshall, George and Cline, Edward F. *You Can't Cheat an Honest Man*. 79 minutes. United States: Universal Pictures, 1939.

Miller, Allan and Smaczny, Paul. *John Cage: Journeys in Sound*. 110 minutes. Leipzig: Accentus Music, 2012.

Minnelli, Vincente. *Gigi*. 115 minutes. United States: Metro-Goldwyn-Mayer, 1958.

Murnau, F. W. *Nosferatu*. 94 minutes. Weimar Republic: Film Arts Guild, 1922.

Neilson, James. *The Scarecrow of Romney Marsh*. In *Walt Disney's Wonderful World of Color*, 129 minutes. United States: Walt Disney Productions, 1964.

Pabst, G. W. *Pandora's Box*. 100 minutes. Weimar Republic: Süd-Film, 1929.

Pabst, G. W. *Diary of a Lost Girl*. 79 minutes. Weimar Republic: Pabst Film, 1929.

Pavlou, George. *Rawhead Rex*. 89 minutes. UK and Ireland: Empire Pictures, 1986.

Perry, Frank. *The Swimmer*. 95 minutes. United States: Columbia Pictures, 1968.

Polanski, Roman. *Repulsion*. 105 minutes. UK: Compton Films and Royal Films International, 1965.

Porter, Edwin S. *The Great Train Robbery*. 12 minutes. United States: Edison Manufacturing Company, 1903.

Powell, Michael. *Peeping Tom*. 101 minutes. UK: Anglo-Amalgamated Film Distributors, 1960.

Preminger, Otto. *Bunny Lake Is Missing*. 107 minutes. UK: Columbia Pictures, 1965.

Reitherman, Wolfgang. *The Jungle Book*. 78 minutes. United States: Buena Vista Distribution, 1967.

Richardson, Clive. *Siouxsie and the Banshees - Once Upon a Time*. 32 minutes. UK: Polygram Video, 1981.

Robertson, John S. *Dr. Jekyll and Mr. Hyde*. 67 minutes. United States: Paramount Pictures, 1920.

Roeg, Nicholas. *Eureka*. 130 minutes. UK: MGM Entertainment Company, 1983.

Romero, George A. *Night of the Living Dead*. 96 minutes. United States: The Walter Reade Organization, 1968.

Rowland, Roy. *The 5000 Fingers of Dr. T*. 92 minutes. United States: Columbia Pictures, 1953.

Russell, Ken. *Peepshow*. 22 minutes. UK, 1956.

Scorsese, Martin. *Taxi Driver*. 113 minutes. United States: Columbia Pictures, 1976.

Serling, Rod. "The Hitch-Hiker." 30 minutes. In *The Twilight Zone*, edited by Rod Serling. United States: CBS Television Distribution, 1960.

Serling, Rod. "The Hitch-Hiker." In *The Twilight Zone*, edited by Rod Serling. United States: CBS Television Distribution, 1960.

Sharman, Jim. *The Rocky Horror Picture Show*. 100 minutes. UK: 20th Century Fox, 1975.

Shindo, Kaneto. *Onibaba*. 103 minutes. Japan: Toho, 1964.

Sternberg, Josef von. *The Blue Angel*. 99 minutes. Weimar Republic: UFA, 1930.

Stevenson, Robert. *Mary Poppins*. 139 minutes. United States: Buena Vista Distribution, 1964.

Suara, Carlos. *Carmen*. 102 minutes. Spain: Emiliano Piedra, Televisión Española, 1983.

Waterhouse, Keith and Hall, Willis. *Worzel Gummidge*. 25 minutes. UK: Southern Television, 1979.

Weinstein, Larry. *Shostakovich against Stalin: The War Symphonies*. 76 minutes. Canada and Germany: Bullfrog Films, 1997.

Whale, James. *Frankenstein*. 71 minutes. United States: Universal Pictures, 1931.

Whale, James. *The Old Dark House*. 71 minutes. United States: Universal Pictures, 1932.

White, James H. *Procession of Mounted Indians and Cowboys*. United States: Edison Manufacturing Company, 1898.

Wickham, Nick. *Siouxsie and the Banshees—the Seven Year Itch: Live at Shepherds Bush Empire.* 88 minutes. UK: Sanctuary Visual Entertainment, 2003.

Wiene, Robert. *Das Cabinet des Dr Caligari.* 74 minutes. Weimar Republic: Decla-Bioscop, 1920.

Wilder, Billy. *Double Indemnity.* 107 minutes. United States: Paramount Pictures, 1944.

Wise, Robert. *The Sound of Music.* 174 minutes. United States: 20th Century Fox, 1965.

Wood, Sam. *A Night at the Opera.* 93 minutes. United States: Metro-Goldwyn-Mayer, 1935.

Wyler, William. *Ben Hur.* 212 minutes. United States: Loew's Inc., 1959.

Wyler, William. *The Collector.* 119 minutes. UK: Columbia Pictures, 1965.

Zinnemann, Fred. *Oklahoma!* 145 minutes. United States: Magna Theatre Corporation, 1955.

Notes

mise en scène

1. John Gibbs, *Mise-En-Scène: Film Style and Interpretation*. London: Wallflower, 2002, p. 5.

2. Gibbs, *Mise-En-Scène*, p. 17.

3. The 1987 Great Storm was one of the UK's worst. On the night of October 16, 1987, an "extreme variant of an extra-tropical cyclone" (Risk Management Solutions Inc. "The Great Storm of 1987: 20-Year Retrospective." London, 2007, p. 3) hit the south east region of England causing immense damage. Bob Prichard stated: "The path of the most ferocious winds spawned earlier in the night had reached all of Sussex, Surrey and Kent, with mean speeds of up to 60kn. By 0400 UTC, there were mean speeds of up to 65kn and many gusts of up to 90kn" (Bob Prichard, "The Great Storm of 16th October 1987." *Weather* 67, No. 10, 2012, p. 256).

4. Marcus K. Harmes, "The Seventeenth Century on Film: Patriarchy, Magistracy and Witchcraft in British Horror Films, 1968-1971." *Canadian Journal of Film Studies* 22, No. 2, 2013, p. 67.

5. Harmes, "The Seventeenth Century on Film," p. 67.

6. Barbara Creed, *The Monstrous-Feminine: Film, Feminism, Psychoanalysis*. London: Routledge, 1993, p. 55.

7. Sioux, in: Anon, "Siouxsie: Me & My Flat." *No1*, No. 145, March 29, 1986, p. 22.

8. In interviews, Sioux often referred to Forbes's *The Stepford Wives*. The Creatures' "So Unreal" was written about the film and Ira Levin's novel of the same name on which the film was based. In an episode of ITV's Video View on Night Network, which aired on July 30, 1988, Sioux describes 1980s band Prefab Sprout as looking ". . . like they've escaped from *The Stepford Wives*. It's my worst nightmare, it's supermarket music." Episode available at: https://www.youtube.com/watch?v=BMrCqLnzZds (accessed February 2018).

9. Sioux, in: Mark Paytress, *Siouxsie and the Banshees: The Authorized Biography*. London: Sanctuary Publishing, 2003, p. 172.

10. Curtis Schwartz, *Pers. Comms.* February 27, 2014.

11. Ibid.

12. Ibid.

13. Budgie, in: Paytress, *Siouxsie and the Banshees*, p. 172.

14. Severin, in: Ibid., p. 172.

15. Klein, in: Ibid., p. 172.

16. Schwartz, *Pers. Comms.*

17. Klein, in: Paytress, *Siouxsie and the Banshees*, p. 171.

18. Sioux, in: Ibid., p. 172.

19. Sioux, in: Lucy O'Brien, "Siouxsie and the Banshees: *A Kiss in the Dreamhouse*." In: *Love Is the Drug—Living as a Pop Fan*, edited by John Aizlewood, 86–99. London: Penguin Books, 1994, p. 94.

20. O'Brien, in: O'Brien, "Siouxsie and the Banshees." p. 94

21. Barbara Creed, *Pandora's Box: Essays in Film Theory*. Victoria: Australian Centre for the Moving Image, 2004, p. 13.

22. Severin, in: Mark Paytress, "Her Dark Materials." *Mojo* 252, November 2014, p. 80.

23. *Peepshow* is not Siouxsie and the Banshees first voyeuristic album title either: *Kaleidoscope*, Polydor, 1980; and, *Through the Looking Glass*, Polydor, 1987 are two further examples.

24. Sioux, in reference to Siouxsie and the Banshees' *Peepshow*. In: Ronnie Randall, "What the Butler Saw!" *Offbeat*, No. 1, September 1988, p. 24.

25. Sioux, in: Ibid.

26. Siouxsie and the Banshees, in: Jean Daniel Beauvallet, "La Fille Fraise." *Les Inrockuptibles*, No. 13, October/November 1988, p. 74.

27. Laura Mulvey, "Visual Pleasure and Narrative Cinema." *Screen* 16, No. 3, 1975, p. 8.

28. Laura Mulvey theorized "the male gaze" in one of the most acclaimed and cited contributions to film theory. See: Mulvey, "Visual Pleasure and Narrative Cinema," p. 11.

29. For more on "trash aesthetics" and paracinema see: Joan Hawkins, *Cutting Edge: Art-Horror and the Horrific Avant-Garde*. Minneapolis: University of Minnesota Press, 2000, pp. 3–7.

30. Ibid., p. 7.

31. Mark Jancovich, *Rational Fears: American Horror in the 1950s*. Manchester: Manchester University Press, 1996, p. 268.

32. Paul Morley, "Siouxsie and the Banshees: A World Domination by 1984 Special." *NME*, January 14, 1978, p. 7.

33. See: Martin Aston, "10 Questions for Siouxsie Sioux." *Mojo*, No. 58, September 1998, pp. 22–23.

34. Ibid.

35. Morley, "Siouxsie and the Banshees," p. 7.

36. David Gavan, "Suburban Relapse: The Birth of the Banshees." *Record Collector* 365, August 2009, p. 37.

37. See: Paul Morley, "Siouxp." *New Musical Express*, November 8, 1980, pp. 28–30; and, Tom Hibbert, "Don't Look Back." Q, No. 26, November 1988, p. 95.

38. Eight of Siouxsie and the Banshees' albums reached the UK album top 20 prior to *Peepshow*. For a comprehensive discography, see Discogs: https://www.discogs.com/artist/80501-Siouxsie-The-Banshees (accessed February 2018).

39. Irene Morra, *Britishness, Popular Music, and National Identity: The Making of Modern Britain*. Routledge Studies in Popular Music. New York: Routledge, 2014, p. 119.

40. Harry Warren and John Mercer, "Jeepers Creepers," 1938. As performed by: Louis Armstrong and his Orchestra. "Jeepers Creepers/What is this Thing Called Swing?" Decca. 1939.

41. Brian Deer, "Workers Rule at the Soho Show." *The Sunday Times*, July 14, 1985. Available at: http://briandeer.com/social/peep-show.htm (accessed February 2018).

42. Sioux, in: Siouxsie and the Banshees, *Downside Up*. EU: Polydor, 2004, p. 57.

43. Sioux, in: Ian Shirley, "Siouxsie and the B-Sides." *Record Collector* 306, January 2005, p. 33.

44. Sioux, in: Tim Nicholson, "Peek-A-Sioux." *Record Mirror*, August 27, 1988, p. 26.

45. Severin, in: Geffen Records, "Peepshow—Press Release." News Release, United States 1988.

46. "The term *film maudit*—literally, "cursed film"—was coined for the legendary 1949 Festival du Film Maudit in Biarritz for which a jury lead by Jean Cocteau curated and celebrated a group of films criminally overlooked and neglected at the time. Today *film maudit* is typically used to designate this latter category of edgy, troubling films and especially the mode of counter-cinema that flourished during the mid-1960s through the late 1970s." Howard Green, "Le Film Maudit." *Harvard Film Archive*. 2009. Available at: http://hcl.harvard.edu/hfa/films/2009julsep/maudit.html (accessed February 2018).

47. Rick Altman, *Film/Genre*. London: British Film Institute, 1999, p. 24.

48. Severin, in: Jarboe, "Steven Severin." *The Living Jarboe*, March 24, 2014. Available at: https://www.thelivingjarboe.com/2014/03/24/steven-severin/ (accessed February 2018).

49. Severin, in: Gavan, "Suburban Relapse," p. 36.

50. Severin, originally at: www.stevenseverin.com 2001 [Website unavailable]. Reprinted in: Peter Routley, *Songs: From the Edge of the World—A Chronological Guide to the Songs of Siouxsie and the Banshees*. iBook. Peter Routley, 2007, p. 464.

51. Severin, in: Geffen Records, "Peepshow—Press Release." Reprinted in: Routley, *Songs*, p. 473.

52. Sioux, in: Jim Shelley, "Ornament of Gold." *NME*, September 24, 1988, p. 19.

53. Sioux, in: Adrian Dannatt, "Goth for It." *Sky Magazine*, No. 26, October 1988, p. 57.

54. Maria Pramaggiore and Tom Wallis, *Film: A Critical Introduction*. 3rd ed. London: Laurence King, 2011, p. 11.

55. Pramaggiore and Wallis, *Film,* pp. 66–67.

56. See: Morley, "Siouxsie and the Banshees," p. 7.

57. Sioux, in: Thomas K. Arnold, "Queen of the Dark Side Finally Sees the Limelight." *Los Angeles Times*, February 11, 1988, p. 2.

58. David Cooper, *Bernard Herrmann's Vertigo: A Film Score Handbook.* Westport, CT and London: Greenwood Press, 2001, p. 31.

59. David Butler, "The Days Do Not End: Film Music, Time and Bernard Herrmann." *Film Studies*, No. 9, Winter 2006, p. 60.

60. Royal Brown, *Overtones and Undertones: Reading Film Music.* Berkeley and London: University of California Press, 1994, p. 13.

61. Ibid.

62. Ibid.

63. Claudia Gorbman, *Unheard Melodies—Narrative Film Music.* Bloomington and Indianapolis: Indiana University Press, 1987, p. 2.

64. Jack Sullivan, *Hitchcock's Music.* New Haven, CT and London: Yale University Press, 2006, p. 18.

65. Mojo Magazine, *It's a Wonderfull Life—A Journey into Sound.* Compiled for Mojo by Siouxsie Sioux and Steven Severin. In: *Mojo* 252, September 30, 2014.

66. Severin, in: Jarboe, "Steven Severin." 2014.

67. Franco Sciannameo, *Nino Rota's The Godfather Trilogy: A Film Score Guide.* Lanham: Scarecrow Press, p. 12.

68. Janina Müller and Tobias Plebuch, "Toward a Prehistory of Film Music: Hans Erdmann's Score for Nosferatu and the Idea of Modular Form." *The Journal of Film Music* 6, No. 1, 2013, p. 37.

69. Friedrich Hollaender b.1896 d.1976 is also known as Frederick Hollander, since he fled Nazi Germany in 1933 and lived in exile in Hollywood, United States before returning to Germany in the 1950s.

70. Trans. "Falling in Love Again (Can't Help It)."

71. Trans. "They Call Me Naughty Lola."

72. In 1998, Sioux and Budgie staged an evening event at The Lux Cinema, London, where they played short extracts from films. During their set, they played two clips from Rowland's *The 5000 Fingers of Dr. T*. The Creatures. "Sioux Records Night." London: The Lux Cinema, Thursday August 27, 1998.

73. Sioux, in: Bracewell, Michael, "Weekend: Her Dark Materials. . ." *The Guardian*, September 24, 2005, p. 40.

74. Ibid.

75. R. Murray Schafer, *The Tuning of the World*. New York: Knopf, 1977, p. 275.

76. Barry Truax, *Acoustic Communication*. Norwood: Ablex Pub. Corp. 1984, p. 207.

77. Alan Williams, "Is Sound Recording Like a Language?" *Yale French Studies*, 60—Cinema/Sound 1980, p. 58.

Early Cinema

1. Brian J. Robb, *Silent Cinema*. Harpenden: Kamera Books, 2007, p. 1.

2. Robb, *Silent Cinema*, p. 2.

3. Severin, in: Sandra A. Garcia, "Siouxsie and the Banshees: Grand Illusions." *BSide*, No. 1, February/March 1989, p. 29.

4. Erkki Huhtamo, "The Pleasures of the Peephole: An Archaeological Exploration of Peep Media." In *Book of Imaginary Media: Excavating the Dream of the Ultimate Communication Medium*, edited by Eric Kluitenberg, 74–155. Rotterdam: NAi Publishers, 2006, p. 98.

5. C. W. Ceram, *Archaeology of the Cinema*. Thames & Hudson, 1965, p. 50.

6. See: Garcia, "Grand Illusions" 1989; Josef Woodard, "Through the Past, Darkly: Siouxsie and the Banshees Ponder a Brighter Tomorrow." *Option*, 1989; and Paytress, "Her Dark Materials."

7. See: Robert V. Adkinson, Hans Janowitz, Carl Writer for the Cinema Mayer, and Robert Wiene, *The Cabinet of Dr. Caligari. A Film by Robert Wiene, Carl Mayer and Hans Janowitz.* English Translation and Description of Action by R. V. Adkinson. London: Lorrimer Publishing, 1972, p. 21.

8. Ibid., p. 24.

9. Intertextuality is a literary and musicological term referring to the relationship between multiple texts. In this case, "Peek-A-Boo" is considered an intertext due to its origin in "Gun" (*Through the Looking Glass*) and that "Gun" in itself was a cover version. The aesthetics of "Peek-A-Boo," as argued in this chapter, also draw upon Weimar aesthetics, therefore the form of the track is considered multi-intertextual.

10. Budgie, in: Randall, "What the Butler Saw!," p. 25.

11. R. N. Dixon-Smith, "G.W. Pabst's Diary of a Lost Girl and the Miracle of Louise Brooks." In G. W. Pabst, "Diary of a Lost Girl." *Weimar Republic*. DVD. 2014 (1929), p. 5.

12. Ibid., p. 6.

13. The album was mixed at Marquee Studios, Soho, where "Catwalk," a B-side of "Peek-A-Boo," was also recorded.

See: Siouxsie and the Banshees, *Downside Up*. EU: Polydor, 2004, p. 57.

14. "Peek-A-Boo" is considered one of Siouxsie and the Banshees best singles. See: Tony Fletcher, "Siouxsie and the Banshees Peep Show." *SPIN*, November 1988, pp. 92–93; Mark Cooper, "Siouxsie and the Banshees—Peepshow." *Q*, 1988, pp. 77–78; and Todd Nakamine, "Siouxsie & the Banshees: The Final Three Studio Albums." *Business Wire*, October 16, 2014. Available at: https://www.businesswire.com/news/home/20141016005894/en/Siouxsie-Banshees-Final-Studio-Albums (accessed February 2018).

15. Mike Hedges, in: Graeme Thomson, "The Music Producers— Part 2: Mike Hedges on Peek-a-Boo by Siouxsie & the Banshees (1988)." *The Word: Home of Intelligent Life on Planet Rock*. [Website unavailable].

16. Sioux, in: Anon, "Word of Mouth: Siouxsie Sioux—Former Banshee, Creature and Now Soloist on Tour." *The Word*, No. 20, October 2004, p. 16.

17. Severin, in: Biba Kopf, "Invisible Jukebox . . . Steven Severin." *The Wire*, 2002.

18. See: Paul Mathur, "Born Again Savages." *Melody Maker*. July 9, 1988, pp. 28–30. He described "Peek-A-Boo" as "thirties hip hop," p. 29.

19. André Hodeir, *Since Debussy: A View of Contemporary Music*. New York: Grove Press, 1961, p. 140.

20. Edith Piaf, "L'Accordioniste." *De L'Accordéoniste à Milord—Vol. 1*. Columbia, 1967.

21. Nakamine, "Siouxsie & the Banshees."

22. Rick Altman, *Silent Film Sound—Film and Culture*. New York: Columbia University Press, 2004, p. 392.

23. This concept in Japanese aesthetics has been applied to music, art, design, and environment, particularly in relation to gardens and landscaping. See: Yuriko Saito, "The Moral Dimension of Japanese Aesthetics." *The Journal of Aesthetics and Art Criticism* 65, No. 1, Winter 2007, p. 90.

24. See: image of Sioux in black, white, and red Japanese kimono on the covers of the *Face* (February 1982) and *Spiral Scratch* (October 1990). Another image of Sioux in a red kimono holding a dish adorned the cover of Japanese magazine *Fool's Mate* (March 1987). Other examples include Sioux pictured in a Hannya mask t-shirt (similar to that featured in Onibaba), the Creatures Japan-inspired *Hái* (2003) among many others.

25. For example, Sioux talked about Onibaba at length and stated "Japanese film amazes me" in: Anon, "Word of Mouth," p. 16. Sioux and Budgie also played a twelve-minute excerpt of *Onibaba* at: The Creatures. "Sioux Records Night." London: The Lux Cinema, Thursday August 27, 1998.

26. Severin, in: David Bowker, "At Their Peek." *International Musician and Recording World*, 1988, p. 29.

27. This effect is normally created using a band-pass filter or what's commonly known as "the telephone effect." In this case, due to the presence of distortion, it is equally likely the result of the old tape recorder as described by Severin.

28. Margaret McCarthy, "Surface Sheen and Charged Bodies: Louise Brooks as Lulu in Pandora's Box (1929)." In *Weimar Cinema: An Essential Guide to Classic Films of the Era*, edited by Noah William Isenberg, 218–36. New York and Chichester: Columbia University Press, 2009, p. 223.

29. Mulvey, "Visual Pleasure and Narrative Cinema," pp. 6–18.

Noir

1. Raymond Borde and Ètienne Chaumeton, "Towards a Definition of *Film Noir*." In *Film Noir Reader*, edited by Alain and Ursini Silver, James, 17–25. New York: Limelight Editions, 1996 (1955), p. 18.

2. Severin, originally at: www.stevenseverin.com 2001 [Website unavailable]. Reprinted in: Routley, *Songs*, 2007, p. 592.

3. Sioux, in: Anon, "Seven Astonishing Facts About Siouxsie (of "And the Banshees" Fame)." *Smash Hits* 10, No. 16, August 10–23, 1988, p. 6.

4. Rick Altman, *Film/Genre*, p. 61.

5. Pramaggiore and Wallis, *Film*, p. 392.

6. Susan Doll and Greg Faller, "Blade Runner and Genre: Film Noir and Science Fiction." *Literature/Film Quarterly* 14, No. 2, 1986, p. 91.

7. Doll and Faller, "Blade Runner and Genre," p. 91.

8. Ibid.

9. Sioux, in: Steve Lafreniere, "Blood Splashed on a Daisy in the Sunshine." *Vice* 15, No. 5, May 2008, p. 131.

10. The single version of "The Killing Jar" features a different arrangement and mix. This chapter focuses on the album version.

11. Michael Atkinson, *Blue Velvet*. London: British Film Institute, 1997, p. 65.

12. Betsy Berry, "Forever in My Dreams: Generic Conventions and the Subversive Imagination in 'Blue Velvet.'" *Literature/Film Quarterly* 16, No. 2, 1988, p. 82.

13. Pete Silverton, "Siouxsie and the Banshees: The Most Elitist Band in the World." *Sounds*, November 25, 1978, p. 31.

14. Borde and Chaumeton, "Towards a Definition of *Film Noir*," p. 22.

15. Severin, in: Peter Routley, *Songs: From the Edge of the World: A Chronological Guide to the Songs of Siouxsie and the Banshees*. iBook, 2007, p. 524.

16. Severin, in: Jon Savage, "Siouxsie and the Banshees: The Unacceptable Face of '78." *Sounds*, June 24, 1978, p. 17.

17. Borde and Chaumeton, "Towards a Definition of *Film Noir*," p. 19.

18. Routley, *Songs: From the Edge of the* World.

19. Severin, originally at: www.stevenseverin.com 2001 [Website unavailable]. Reprinted in: Routley, *Songs*, 2007, p. 592.

20. Byron Haskin, "Demon with a Glass Hand." In *The Outer Limits*, edited by Leslie Stevens, 51 minutes. United States: ABC, 1964.

21. James Wierzbicki notes the "golden age" of film music in Hollywood between 1933 and 1949. See: James Eugene Wierzbicki, *Film Music—A History*. New York: Routledge, 2009, p. 133.

22. Kathryn Marie Kalinak, *Film Music: A Very Short Introduction*. New York: Oxford University Press, 2010, p. 65.

23. Claudia Gorbman, *Unheard Melodies—Narrative Film Music*. Bloomington and Indianapolis: Indiana University Press, 1987, p. 4.

24. "Needles and Pins," although written by Jack Nitzsche and Sonny Bono for Jackie DeShannon in 1963, is a much-covered classic—versions by the Searchers (1964), the Ramones

(1978) and Tom Petty (1985) were more successful than DeShannon's original.

25. Sioux, in: Steve Malins, "Across the Tracks—Siouxsie and the Banshees." *Vox (Record Hunter)*, No. 27, 1992, pp. 8–9.

26. For a more detailed analysis of reverb in this track, see: Samantha Bennett, "Time-based Signal Processing and Shape in Alternative Rock Recordings." *iaspm@journal* 6, No. 2, 2016.

27. As discussed in: Frank Krutnik, *In a Lonely Street: Film Noir, Genre, Masculinity*. London and New York: Routledge, 2006, p. x.

28. Kathrin Fahlenbrach, "Emotions in Sound: Audiovisual Metaphors in the Sound Design of Narrative Films." *Projections* 2, No. 2, 2008, p. 86.

29. Ibid.

30. The Holy Bible: King James Version. *Genesis 3.19* Peabody, MA: Hendrickson Bibles. 2011, p. 2.

31. David Bowie, "Ashes to Ashes" *Scary Monsters (And Super Creeps)* RCA, 1980.

Musical

1. Severin, in: Mark Paytress, "Her Dark Materials," p. 80.

2. Altman, *Film/Genre*, p. 32.

3. Pramaggiore and Wallis, *Film*, p. 398.

4. Kevin Jackson, *Nosferatu—Eine Symphonie Des Grauens*. Bfi Film Classics, edited by British Film Institute London: BFI Palgrave, 2013, p. 88.

5. Leon Hunt, "Necromancy in the UK: Witchcraft and the Occult in British Horror." In *British Horror Cinema*, edited by Steve Chibnall, 82–98. London and New York: Routledge, 2002, p. 96.

6. Severin, originally at: www.stevenseverin.com 2001 [Website unavailable]. Reprinted in: Routley, *Songs*, p. 464.

7. Robert H. Bell, "Implicated without Choice: The Double Vision of *the Singing Detective*." *Literature/ Film Quarterly* 21, No. 3, 1993, p. 208.

8. C. Kenneth Pellow, "The Function of 'The Bloody Songs' in Dennis Potter's *The Singing Detective*." *The Journal of Popular Culture* 46, No. 5, 2013, p. 1051.

9. Siouxsie and the Banshees, *Peepshow*. Polydor, 1988.

10. Hugh Rockoff, "The 'Wizard of Oz' as a Monetary Allegory." *The Journal of Political Economy* 98, No. 4, 1990, p. 746.

11. Ibid.

12. T. S. Eliot, *T.S. Eliot—The Complete Poems and Plays*. Orlando: Harcourt Brace & Company, 1950, p. 56.

13. The connection between *The Wizard of Oz* and Eliot's *The Hollow Men* is made by Salman Rushdie, *The Wizard of Oz*. Bfi Film Classics, edited by British Film Institute. 2nd ed. London: BFI Palgrave, 2012, p. 49.

14. The tale of Rumpelstiltskin originated in Germany and is thought to be thousands of years old. The first publication of the tale was made in 1812, where it featured in *Grimm's Fairytales*.

15. Rick Altman, *The American Film Musical*. Bloomington: Indiana University Press, 1987, p. 28.

16. Ibid.

17. Ibid., p. 31.

18. Ibid., p. 32.

19. Kay Dickinson, *Movie Music, the Film Reader*. London: Routledge, 2003, p. 3.

20. Altman, *The American Film Musical*, p. 45.

21. Ibid., p. 50.

22. Rudolf Kuenzli, *Dada and Surrealist Film*. Cambridge, MA and London: The MIT Press, 1996, p. 10.

23. Severin, originally at: www.stevenseverin.com 2001 [Website unavailable]. Reprinted in: Routley, *Songs*, p. 464.

24. David Bowie, "The Bewlay Brothers." *Hunky Dory* RCA, 1971.

25. Severin, originally at: www.stevenseverin.com 2001 [Website unavailable]. Reprinted in: Routley, *Songs*, p. 464.

Vaudeville

1. See: Gilbert Chase, *America's Music, from the Pilgrims to the Present. Music in American Life*. 3rd ed. Urbana: University of Illinois Press, 1987, pp. 364–65.

2. Lauren Rabinovitz, *For the Love of Pleasure: Women, Movies, and Culture in Turn-of-the-Century Chicago*. New Brunswick, NJ and London: Rutgers University Press, 1998, p. 138.

3. John F. Kasson, *Amusing the Million: Coney Island at the Turn of the Century*, 1978, p. 49.

4. Thomas A. Edison, "Merry-Go-Round" United States, September 3, 1898. For further details, see: Charles Musser. *Edison Motion Pictures, 1890-1900—An Annotated*

Filmography. Washington DC: Smithsonian Institution Press, 1997, #620, p. 466.

5. Carousel comes from the French *carrousel*, and the merry-go-round features in Stevens's 1729 poem on St. Bartholomew's Fair. For more details on the history of the carousel, see: Frederick Fried, *A Pictorial History of the Carousel*. New York: A. S. Barnes, 1964, pp. 18–19.

6. See: A. Nicholas Vardac, *Stage to Screen: Theatrical Method from Garrick to Griffith*. Cambridge, MA: Harvard University Press, 1949, p. 182.

7. This separation of film from vaudeville took place in 1905. Harry Davis, a successful theater manager, pioneered the nickelodeon: a theater dedicated to the projection of moving pictures. See: Lauren Rabinovitz, *Electric Dreamland: Amusement Parks, Movies, and American Modernity*. New York: Columbia University Press, 2012, p. 6.

8. W. C. Fields was one of Sioux's favorite and most cited film actors. See: R. Harrington, "All's Wail With Siouxsie." *The Washington Post*. May 12, 1986; and Shelley, "Ornament of Gold," p. 19.

9. Trav, S. D., *No Applause, Just Throw the Money: The Book That Made Vaudeville Famous*. New York: Faber and Faber, 2005, p. 119.

10. The influence of Disney on Siouxsie and the Banshees runs deep. A few examples of dozens more that exist include: the band's cover of "Trust in Me" taken from Disney's "The Jungle Book" (1967) and featured on their album *Through the Looking Glass* (1986); The lyrical reference to Peter Pan in "Are You Still Dying, Darling?" (B-Side to "The Killing Jar" (1988)); the inclusion of music from Disney's *Fantasia* on the 2014 Mojo cover CD *It's a Wonderfull Life* and in the Creatures'

"Sioux Records Night" at Lux Cinema, London, 1988; and, the inclusion of "When You Wish Upon A Star" taken from Disney's *Pinocchio* (1940), again on the 2014 Mojo cover CD *It's a Wonderfull Life*.

11. Siouxsie and the Banshees, "The Killing Jar" b/w "Something Wicked This Way Comes" "Are You Still Dying, Darling?" Polydor, September 30, 1988.

12. Severin, in: Garcia, "Siouxsie and the Banshees," p. 37.

13. Ibid.

14. Serling, "The Twilight Zone."

15. Sioux, in: Shelley, "Ornament of Gold," p. 19.

16. Severin, in: Garcia, "Grand Illusions," p. 37.

17. Adkinson, et al., *The Cabinet of Dr. Caligari*, p. 23.

18. See: Tom Gunning, "The Cinema of Attraction: Early Film, Its Spectator and the Avant-Garde." *Wide Angle* 8, 1986, pp. 3–4.

19. Gunning, "The Cinema of Attraction," p. 73.

20. Sergei Eisenstein, "How I Became A Film Director." In *Notes of a Film Director*. Moscow: Foreign Language Publishing House, p. 16.

21. Sergei Eisenstein, "Montage of Attractions." Trans. Daniel Gerould. In *The Drama Review*. 18, No. 1, 1974, pp. 78–79.

22. Gunning is clear in his attribution of the cinema of attractions to Eisenstein, as he states, "The term attractions refers backwards to a popular tradition and forwards to an avant-garde subversion. The tradition is that of the fairground and carnival, and particularly its development during the turn of the century in such modern amusement parks as Coney Island. The avant-garde radicalization of this term comes in the theoretical and practical work in theatre and film of Sergei Eisenstein,

whose theory of the montage of attractions intensified this popular energy into an aesthetic subversion, through a radical theorization of the power of attractions to undermine the conventions of bourgeois realism." In Tom Gunning, "An Aesthetic of Astonishment: Early Film and the (In)Credulous Spectator." *Art and Text* 34, Spring 1989, pp. 31–45.

23. Gunning, "Now You See It, Now You Don't: The Temporality of the Cinema of Attractions," 1996, p. 73.

24. Ibid., p. 75.

25. Ibid.

26. Sioux, in: Steve Morse, "Siouxsie & the Banshees: No Run-of-the-Mill Band." *Boston Globe*, October 21, 1988, p. 61.

27. Budgie, in: Paytress, *Siouxsie and the Banshees*, p. 178.

28. Altman, *Silent Film Sound*, p. 104.

29. This synthesized introductory line first appears hard right with a delayed copy appearing hard left momentarily after.

30. Cage, in: Allan Miller and Paul Smaczny, "John Cage: Journeys in Sound." 110 minutes. Leipzig: Accentus Music, 2012.

31. Sioux, in: Budgie, in: Paytress, *Siouxsie and the Banshees*, p. 172. During pre-production sessions at Ardingly, Siouxsie and the Banshees visited nearby Lindfield for bonfire night (November 5, 1987) and also a local "gypsy fairground." Siouxsie also stated "I do most of my work on a Dictaphone. I don't need any technology. Anything I can turn on and off is fine with me, the simpler the better." In Woodard, "Through the Past, Darkly," p. 42.

32. Alfred Hitchcock, *Vertigo*. United States: Paramount Pictures, 1958.

33. See: Cooper, *Bernard Herrmann's Vertigo*, p. 76.

34. Woodard, "Through the Past, Darkly," p. 41.

35. A vibraslap is a percussion instrument played by striking a wooden ball connected to a metal spiral and a wooden board. In this case, the vibraslap is synthesized—its envelope on the recording is too long for it to be an acoustic instrument.

36. Jon Klein discussed his guitar rig in detail in: Tony Reed, "Control Zone: Peepshow People." *Melody Maker*, 1988, September 24, 1988, p. 60.

37. This sound appears to be percussive and metallic at first, however, listening through 2.33–2.39, the sound's components morph into a "swoosh" ascending in pitch. This is consistent with the manual adjusting of filter controls on an analogue synthesizer.

Western

1. Sioux, in: Woodard, "Through the Past, Darkly," p. 42.

2. Ibid.

3. Ibid.

4. Budgie, in: Ibid.

5. Sioux, in: Ibid.

6. Ibid.

7. Joel Dinerstein, *Swinging the Machine: Modernity, Technology, and African American Culture between the World Wars.* Amherst and Boston: University of Massachusetts Press, 2003, p. 67.

8. B. S. Brown, "Hale's Tours and Scenes of the World." *The Moving Picture World July 1916.* New York: Chalmers Publishing Company, July 15, 1916, p. 372.

9. Russell Merritt, "Nickelodeon Theatres, 1905-1914: Building an Audience for the Movies." In *Hollywood: Critical Concepts in Media and Cultural Studies, Volume 1*, edited by T. Schatz. London and New York: Routledge, 2004, pp. 25–41.

10. Raymond Fielding, "Hale's Tours: Ultrarealism in the Pre-1910 Motion Picture." *Society for Cinema and Media Studies* 10, No. 1, 1970, p. 43.

11. Ibid.

12. Martin Loiperdinger and Bernd Elzer, "Lumiere's Arrival of the Train: Cinema's Founding Myth." *The Moving Image* 4, No. 1, 2004, p. 92.

13. Daryl E. Jones, "The Earliest Western Films." *Journal of Popular Film and Television* 8, No. 2, 1980, p. 42.

14. Alison Griffiths, "Playing at Being Indian: Spectatorship and the Early Western." *Journal of Popular Film & Television* 29, No. 3, 2001, pp. 100–11.

15. Ibid.

16. Jones, "The Earliest Western Films," p. 42.

17. Jacquelyn Kilpatrick, *Celluloid Indians: Native Americans and Film*. Lincoln and London: University of Nebraska Press, p. xvii.

18. Sioux played down the connection between her stage name and Sioux Indians, instead citing a letter sign off—'s x'—as the inspiration behind her name change. See Paytress, *Siouxsie and the Banshees*, p. 38.

19. Sioux, in: Shelley, "Ornament of Gold," p. 19.

20. Pramaggiore and Wallis, *Film*, p. 388.

21. Gorbman, *Unheard Melodies—Narrative Film Music*, p. 3.

22. Budgie, in: Bowker, "At Their Peek," p. 29.

23. Victor Kennedy, *Strange Brew: Metaphors of Magic and Science in Rock Music.* Cambridge: Cambridge Scholars Publishing, 2013, p. 16.

24. Dinerstein, *Swinging the Machine,* p. 88.

25. Brown, *Overtones and Undertones,* p. 345.

26. Kenneth LaFave, *Experiencing Film Music: A Listener's Companion.* Lanham, MD: Rowman & Littlefield, 2017, p. 81.

27. Pramaggiore and Wallis, *Film,* p. 388.

28. Severin, in: Paytress, "Her Dark Materials," p. 80.

29. Shelley, "Ornament of Gold," p. 19.

30. The Crickets, "Oh Boy!" b/w "Not Fade Away" 1957 Brunswick Radio Corporation; and The Rolling Stones. "Not Fade Away" b/w "Little by Little" 1964 Decca.

31. There are multiple references to fire and brimstone throughout the old and new testaments. See: The Holy Bible: King James Version. Peabody, MA: Hendrickson Bibles. 2011: Gen. 19:24 (p. 9), Isa. 30:33 (pp. 343–44), Job 18:15 (p. 266) and St. Lk. 17:29 (p. 500).

32. Yechiel Szeintuch, "The Myth of the Salamander in the Work of Ka-Tzetnik." *Partial Answers: Journal of History and the History of Ideas* 3, No. 1, 2005, p. 103.

33. According to Albert Jack, author of *Pop Goes the Weasel: The Secret Meanings of Nursery Rhymes*, the rhyme "Jack be Nimble" was first published in 1798, although its origins date back much further.

34. Dinerstein, *Swinging the Machine,* p. 87.

35. Severin, in: Sandra A. Garcia, "Grand Illusions." *BSide,* February 1989, p. 28.

Fantasy

1. Sioux, in: Polydor, "Peepshow—Press Kit." News Release, 1988.

2. Ibid.

3. See: Lynn E. Roller, "The Legend of Midas." *Classical Antiquity* 2, No. 2, 1983, pp. 299–317.

4. Richard M. Krill, "Midas: Fact and Fiction." *International Social Science Review* 59, No. 1, 1984, p. 32.

5. Miriam Robbins Dexter, "The Ferocious and the Erotic: 'Beautiful' Medusa and the Neolithic Bird and Snake." *Journal of Feminist Studies in Religion* 26, No. 1, 2010, p. 26.

6. Charlotte Currie, "Transforming Medusa." *Amaltea. Revisita de Mitocritica* 3, 2011, p. 170.

7. Susan T. Stevens, "Charon's Obol and Other Coins in Ancient Funerary Practice." *Phoenix* 45, No. 3, 1991, p. 215.

8. Roger Scruton, "Fantasy, Imagination and the Screen." *Grazer Philosophische Studien* 19, No. 1, 1983, p. 42.

9. Scruton, "Fantasy, Imagination and the Screen." p. 45.

10. Katherine A. Fowkes, *The Fantasy Film*. Chichester, UK: Wiley Blackwell, 2010, p. 1.

11. Ibid., p. 2.

12. Sioux, in: Mark Copper, "Banshee of the Innocents." *The Guardian*, September 16, 1988, p. 31.

13. Timothy D. Taylor, *Beyond Exoticism*. Durham and London: Duke University Press, 2007, p. 2.

14. Ibid.

15. Ibid., p. 9.

16. Sioux, in: Shelley, "Ornament of Gold," p. 19.

17. Ibid.

18. N. J. Dawood, *The Koran* (43:32), p. 345.

19. Ibid. (43:35) p. 345.

20. Ibid. (43:74) p. 347.

21. The Holy Bible: King James Version. *Daniel 3: 4-6* Peabody, MA: Hendrickson Bibles, 2011, p. 422.

22. Curt Sachs, *The History of Musical Instruments.* Mineola and New York: Dover Publications Inc., 2006, p. 258.

23. Reed, "Control Zone," p. 60.

24. A listen through the presets on all these instruments corroborates this. While there are many similar sounding patches on the DX-7 and Mirage, none are a perfect match to the sounds used on "Ornaments of Gold."

25. Reed, "Control Zone," p. 60.

26. Scruton, "Fantasy, Imagination and the Screen," p. 46.

27. N. J. Dawood, *The Koran* (Translated from the Arabic.) Rev. Ed. Ed. London: Penguin, 2003, p. 347.

28. McCarrick, in: Reed, "Control Zone," p. 61.

29. Steve Sutherland, "Blood Sport." *Melody Maker*, October 7, 1989, p. 10.

30. Bowker, "At Their Peek," p. 29.

31. Budgie, in: Adam Budofsky, "Budgie." *Modern Drummer*, 1990, pp. 29–31, 110–14.

32. Stevens, "Charon's Obol and Other Coins in Ancient Funerary Practice," p. 215.

Horror

1. Sioux, in: Charles Mueller, "Gothicism and English Goth Music: Notes on the Repertoire," 2012, p. 77. Quote originally printed in: Dave Thompson, *The Dark Reign of Gothic Rock.* London: Helter Skelter Publishing, 2002, p. 45.

2. Siouxsie and the Banshees, "Spellbound," *Juju* Polydor, 1981.

3. Siouxsie and the Banshees, "Playground Twist," *Join Hands* Polydor, 1979.

4. Siouxsie and the Banshees, "Candyman," *Tinderbox* Polydor, 1986.

5. Sioux, in: Biba Kopf, "The Sweetest Chill." *NME*, September 28, 1985, p. 34.

6. Clive Barker, *Books of Blood—Volume III*. London: Sphere, 1984.

7. Alessandro Calovolo, "Vaghe Stelle della Maharani." *Rockerilla*, No. 98, Ottobre 1988, p. 11. With thanks to Costas Christopodoulos for translating this quote.

8. The first mention of Rawhead and Bloody Bones is found in Gascoigne's mid-sixteenth-century play *Wyll the Devyll* (c. 1550).

9. Archer Taylor. "Raw Head and Bloody Bones." *The Journal of American Folklore* 69, No. 272, 1956, p. 114.

10. Ibid.

11. See: Eliza Gutch, *Examples of Printed Folk-lore Concerning Lincolnshire*, 1908, p. 58.

12. See: Elizabeth Wright, *Rustic Speech and Folklore*. Oxford: Oxford University Press, 1913, p. 119.

13. Ibid.

14. S. E. Schlosser, *Raw head and Bloodybones: A Missouri Ghost Story,* 2010. Available at: http://americanfolklore.net/folklore/2010/07/raw_head_and_bloody_bones.html (accessed February 2018).

15. Stan Link, "The Monster and the Music Box: Children and the Soundtrack of Horror." In *Music in the Horror Film—Listening to Fear,* edited by Neil Lerner, 38–54. New York: Routledge, 2010, p. 43.

16. Nancy Thompson is a much-studied cinematic protagonist. For example, John Kenneth Muir draws parallels between Nancy's heroic character and Shakespeare's Hamlet since both are focused on stamping out the lies of their mothers. See: J. K. Muir, *Horror Films of the 1980s.* Jefferson: McFarland & Company, 2007, p. 19.

17. Linda Williams, "When the Woman Looks." In *Re-Vision: Essays in Feminist Film Criticism,* edited by Mary Ann. Doane, Mellencamp, Patricia, Williams, Linda. The American Film Institute Monograph Series, 83–89. Los Angeles: University Publications of America, 1984, p. 88.

18. Richard J. Anobile, ed. *James Whale's Frankenstein Starring Boris Karloff,* The Film Classics Library. London: Picador, 1974, p. 6.

19. Steve Fisk, in: *Can't Look Away: The Lure of Horror Film.* Experience Music Project Museum (EMP) Seattle, WA, 2016.

20. Ibid.

21. Klein discussed his guitar rig at length in both: Reed, "Control Zone," p. 60; and, Bowker, "At Their Peek," pp. 24–29.

22. The Harmonizer was a classic pitch-shifting delay processor made by Eventide and a common system in recording studios throughout the 1980s. Jon Klein spoke about incorporating the Harmonizer into the guitar chain in: Reed, "Control Zone," p. 61.

23. Ibid.

24. Creed, *The Monstrous-Feminine*, p. 56.

25. A pre-delay is a time-based signal processing effect applied to increase the distance between a direct signal and its first reflections. It distances the reverb from the direct signal (in this case, the voice) allowing for a clearer, more "present" vocal.

26. Mary Ann Doane, "Scale and the Negotiation of 'Real' and 'Unreal' Space in the Cinema." Chap. 5. In *Realism and the Audiovisual Media*, edited by Lucia Nagib and Cecilia Mello, 63–84. Basingstoke: Palgrave Macmillan, 2009, p. 78.

27. Michel Chion and Claudia Gorbman, *Audio-Vision: Sound on Screen* (in Translation of: L'audio-vision. Paris: Editions Nathan, c1990.). New York: Columbia University Press, 1994, p. 221.

Epic

1. Vivian Sobchack, "'Surge and Splendor': A Phenomenology of the Hollywood Historical Epic." *Representations* 29, Winter 1990, p. 28.

2. Ibid.

3. Severin, in: Paytress, "Her Dark Materials," p. 84. In reference to "The Last Beat of My Heart."

4. Tom Brown, "Spectacle/Gender/History: The Case of *Gone with the Wind*." *Screen* 49, No. 2, Summer 2008, p. 159.

5. Ibid.

6. Ibid., p. 157.

7. Ibid.

8. Sioux, in: Cathi Unsworth, "Interview: Twice Upon a Time." *Melody Maker*, October 17, 1992, p. 8.

9. Siouxsie and the Banshees, *Downside Up*. EU: Polydor, 2004, p. 51.

10. Linda Williams, "Melodrama Revised." In *Refiguring American Film Genres: History and Theory*, edited by Nick Browne. Berkeley: University of California Press, 1998, p. 42.

11. Ibid., p. 65.

12. J. R. R Tolkien, *The Fellowship of the Ring: Being the First Part of the Lord of the Rings*. Oxford: George Allen & Unwin, 1954.

13. Severin, originally at: www.stevenseverin.com 2001 [Website unavailable]. Reprinted in: Routley, *Songs*, 2007, p. 579.

14. Linda Williams, "Melodrama Revised," p. 66.

15. Severin, originally at: www.stevenseverin.com 2001 [Website unavailable]. Reprinted in: Routley, *Songs*, 2007, p. 579.

16. Linda Williams, "Melodrama Revised," p. 67.

17. Brown, "Spectacle/Gender/History," p. 165.

18. Fleming, *Gone with the Wind*.

19. Woodard, "Through the Past, Darkly," p. 44.

20. Brown, "Spectacle/Gender/History," p. 177.

21. Thomas Elsaesser, "Tales of Sound and Fury: Observations on the Family Melodrama." *Monogram* 4, 1972, pp. 2–15. Reprinted in: *Home Is Where the Heart Is: Studies in Melodrama and the Woman's Film*, edited by Christine Gledhill. London: BFI, p. 66.

22. Sioux, in: Lois Wilson, "Dark Stuff." *Mojo* [Collections], No. 105, August 2002, p. 154.

23. Williams, "Melodrama Revised," p. 69.

24. Ibid.

25. Sioux, in: Kris Needs, "Haul of Mirrors." *ZigZag*, May 1980, pp. 4–5.

26. Paul Allen Anderson, "The World Heard: *Casablanca* and the Music of War." *Critical Inquiry,* Spring 2006, p. 497.

27. Phil Powrie, "The Fabulous Destiny of the Accordion in French Cinema." In *Changing Tunes: The Use of Pre-Existing Music in Film*, edited by Phil Powrie. Aldershot: Ashgate, 2006, p. 137.

28. Anderson, "The World Heard," p. 497.

29. Brown, "Spectacle/Gender/History," p. 167.

30. Ibid.

31. Sobchack, "'Surge and Splendor,'" p. 25.

32. Sioux, in: Shelley, "Ornament of Gold," p. 19.

33. Solomon Volkov, *Testimony: The Memoirs of Dmitri Shostakovich*. Twenty Fifth Anniversary Edition. New Jersey: Limelight Editions, 2004.

34. Ibid., p. xv.

35. Elizabeth Wilson, *Shostakovich: A Life Remembered*. Princeton, NJ: Princeton University Press, 1994, p. xi.

36. Ibid.

37. It must be noted that at the time "Rhapsody" was written, Volkov's *Testimony*—and other readings on Shostakovich's life—shared this perspective. Wilkinson's book, a more balanced reappraisal, was first published in 1994.

38. Sioux, in: Anon, "Heroes" *Melody Maker*, October 1, 1988, p. 36.

39. Budgie, in: Budofsky, "Budgie," pp. 29–31, 110–14.

40. Mariana Sabanina, in: Larry Weinstein, "Shostakovich against Stalin: The War Symphonies." 76 minutes. Canada and Germany: Bullfrog Films, 1997.

41. Wilson, *Shostakovich,* p. 120.

42. Ibid., p. 126.

43. Rubinin: Weinstein, "Shostakovich against Stalin."

44. John Riley, *Dmitri Shostakovich: A Life in Film*. London: I. B. Tauris, 2005, p. 70.

45. Riley, *Dmitri Shostakovich*, p. 66.

46. Sobchack, "'Surge and Splendor,'" p. 29.

47. Constantine Santas, *The Epic in Film: From Myth to Blockbuster*. Lanham, MD: Rowman & Littlefield Publishers, Inc., 2008, pp. 29–32.

48. Severin, in: Biba Kopf, "Invisible Jukebox . . . Steven Severin." *The Wire*, No. 198, August 2000, p. 36.

49. Santas, *The Epic in Film*, p. 30.

50. Wilson, *Shostakovich*, p. 424.

51. Ibid.

52. Olga Dombrovskaia, "Hamlet, King Lear and Their Companions: The Other Side of Film Music." *Contemplating Shostakovich: Life, Music and Film*, edited by Alexander, Ivashkin and Kirkman, Andrew, 141–64. Farnham: Ashgate, 2012, p. 161.

53. Derek C. Hulme, *Dmitri Shostakovich Catalogue: The First Hundred Years and Beyond*. Lanham, MD: The Scarecrow Press, 2010, p. 531.

54. Sioux, in: Sioux, in: Lafreniere, "Blood Splashed on a Daisy in the Sunshine," p. 131.

55. Linda Alchin, *The Secret History of Nursery Rhymes*. London: Babyseen Ltd, 2010, p. 41.

56. Ibid.

57. Rudolf Arnheim, "Epic and Dramatic Film." *Film Culture* 3, No. 1, 1957, p. 9.

58. Brown, "Spectacle/Gender/History," p. 159.

59. Robb, *Silent Cinema*, p. 103.

60. Richard Taylor, *The Battleship Potemkin: The Film Companion*. London: I. B. Tauris, 2000, p. 35.

61. Taylor, *The Battleship Potemkin*, p. 41.

62. Tom Armstrong, "Response: Music, Image and the Sublime." *Textual Practice* 22, No. 1, 2008, p. 77.

63. Ibid.

64. Severin, in: Geffen Records, "Peepshow—Press Release."

65. Taylor, *Beyond Exoticism*, p. 4.

66. Sioux, in: Paytress, *Siouxsie and the Banshees*, p. 78.

Also available in the series